Ice Luminary Magic

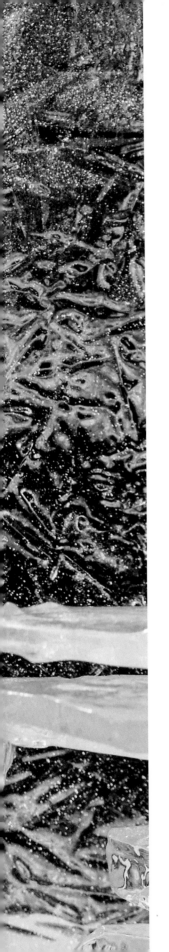

Ice Luminary Magic

The Ice Wrangler's Guide
to Making Illuminated Ice Creations

Jennifer Shea Hedberg

Tom Hedberg lights candles in the base of an ice bar in preparation for a winter gathering. — *Photo by Bob Hays*

For Tom,
my husband, "senior staff iceologist," sounding board
and the one who says, "Sure, set up a water sprinkler
in the backyard in the middle of winter.
Sounds like a good idea."

For Frances Ann Seals Shea,
my mother, who fostered my creative spirit.

And for the photographers,
who have captured the beauty of ice over the years.
This book would not exist without you.

The following photographers and ice artists
contributed to Ice Luminary Magic:

Martha Shull Archer
Mary Arneson
Per Breiehagen
John Breitinger
Todd Buchanan
Bruce Challgren
Mark Clingan
Natasha D'Schommer
Rob Enedy
David Falk
Kalyn Falk
Jana Freiband
Shane Foss
Stephen L. Garrett
Patrick Groleau
Bob Hays

Elizabeth Shea Hedberg
Dale Hammerschmidt
Tom Hedberg
Lauri Hohman
Kathy Loeffler
Nettie Magnuson
Gail Murton
Rob Nopola
Pat Palanuk
Ashley Rick
Larry Risser
Efrén Solanas
Becky Stolinas
Jim Young

— *Photo by Bruce Challgren*

Contents

Introduction

A few years back Minnesota journalist Chris Lee spent the evening with me as I put the finishing touches on an ice installation. She described what she saw in an article in *Midwest Home* magazine:

> *That time between sunset and dark on cold Minnesota days is magical. Even when the air is so sharp it cuts, it softens ever so slightly as the indigo twilight approaches.*
>
> *This is the moment when ice lanterns lit from within begin to show their stuff: 30-pound spheres of crystallized water glow against snowy landscapes, their lacy intricacies and star-burst patterns coming to life as night falls. Their beauty is so compelling that even their creator, Jennifer Shea Hedberg, pauses to observe the impact of her work.*
>
> *This is why she does it. These ethereal scenes are her payoff for spending hours in the cold, forming ice into shapes that range from simple frozen orbs to fragile spears that sparkle and gleam like fine, carved crystal. Only the process of freezing wields the knife, however; Hedberg simply manipulates it.*

There's a magic in working with ice and light, and Chris brought it to life with her words. This is the same quiet mystery that inspires my work and moves me to share it with others. Over the last three decades I've come to understand how to guide the freezing of water, how to wrangle creations from ice and how to light them from within to release their beauty. This book offers simple instruction in what I call "Ice Logic" — the basic principles I've distilled through years of practice — and then puts that logic into practice in step-by-step illustrated ice luminary projects. Look for these symbols to discover each project's level of difficulty:

 Easy    Intermediate    Challenging    Advanced

The ideal way to use this book is to soak up some Ice Logic, tackle a few of the starter projects and then try your hand at the exciting projects that follow. It's my hope that this book will move you to create delightful ice luminaries of your own and share their beauty with others.

Enjoy the glow!

Jennifer Shea Hedberg

Above: Ice luminaries and sculptures light up a front walkway. — Photo by Todd Buchanan, Midwest Home magazine

PART 1: Ice Logic

A Story of Ice and Flame

Since the beginning of time, winter has been a time for festivals of light. From the lantern festivals of ancient China and the Hindu celebration of Diwali to the Scandinavian celebration of St. Lucia's Day, kindling light in the dark is the human way.

Here in the cold north, people light up the dark with ice lanterns — translucent shells of frozen water sheltering a glowing flame. It's one way of stoking the cozy feeling the Danish call hygge, *which calls for rejoicing in winter rather than grimly enduring it. Lighting up the landscape with ice lanterns requires little more than a willingness to experiment and some basic knowledge of the logic of water and ice. Once you understand how this amazing substance "thinks," you'll know how to coax it into globes, wrap it around flowers, conjure it into "glass" and stretch it into towers.*

This book explores both the art and the science of working with ice — beginning with the simplicity of a hollow chunk of frozen water. It's an exhilarating story, and I'm delighted to share it with you.

LUMINARIA: A paper bag weighed down with sand, lit by a candle within

ICE LANTERN or ICE LUMINARY: A shell of ice shielding a candle from wind, snow and rain.

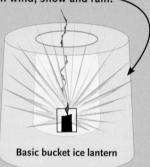

Basic bucket ice lantern

ICE LUMINARY SCULPTURE: A configuration of ice glass and/ or ice lanterns illuminated with a candle or LED lights.

Freezing Water, Shaping Ice

Ice Lantern Basics

Making an ice lantern is nearly as simple as filling a form with water and setting it out to freeze. Choose a balloon, a bucket, or even an upside-down traffic cone — anything that can withstand the expansion that occurs as water becomes ice — and you're mostly there. All that remains is to choose a freezing strategy that will create a cavity for a light source within the lantern.

Nature and human ingenuity can help. The easiest approach involves relying on water's inclination to freeze from the outside in, but allowing the water to solidify only long enough to form a sturdy shell — and then removing the ice from the container to release the unfrozen water from its core. Another technique entails freezing a container's water all the way through — but only after positioning a smaller shape inside to create a hollow area at the center. Both techniques work fine, but there's something to love about letting nature do the work — as the partial-freeze method does.

Ice Wrangler installation at the City of Lakes Luminary Loppet in Minneapolis.
— Photo by Stephen L. Garrett

Water Logic — *The Science Behind the Magic*

Creating with ice isn't just an art. It's also simple science. Nearly all ice luminary creations involve freezing water in containers, and water changes as it takes solid form. Before diving into the artistry, it's essential to understand the logic of water. Let's have a look.

START WITH SAFETY

Working with water in freezing temps can be dangerous. Make sure you're prepared before you venture outside.

Dress wisely. When handling water and exerting yourself in freezing temps, wear clothing appropriate for winter activity. Dress in layers and remember, "cotton is rotten."

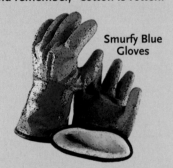

Smurfy Blue Gloves

Ice is slippery, cold and heavy. When handling it, I wear insulated, waterproof gloves — I call them "Smurfy Blues" — to keep my hands warm and dry. In a pinch, rubber dishwashing gloves worn over wool liners work well, too.

My favorite Smurfy Blues are available at wintercraft.com.

Caution! If you get wet while working in the cold, seek shelter and change clothes immediately!

Water Is Sticky

A candle's flame inside an ice lantern slowly melts the walls of the inner cavity. Because water molecules like to stick to each other, the melting ice runs down the sides of the lantern instead of falling straight down and dousing the flame.

Why? A water molecule consists of three atoms: one oxygen (-) and two hydrogen (+).

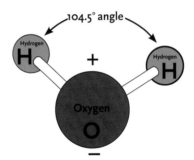

104.5° angle

Hydrogen H   +   Hydrogen H

Oxygen O

−

When water molecules are near each other, they want to pull together. The positive hydrogen-heavy side of one water molecule is always drawn to the negative oxygen-only side of another water molecule. This is called a hydrogen bond.

Water Expands as It Freezes

If water in a container is allowed to freeze solid, not only will the container probably break, but the ice created will have large cracks running through it and be structurally unsound. If some water is removed before it freezes solid, the ice will be strong.

Why? When water molecules are warm and their energy level is high, they move constantly—bonding together and breaking apart frequently.

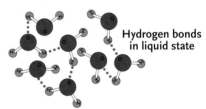

Hydrogen bonds in liquid state

When water begins to freeze, its energy level drops and hydrogen molecules are able to connect in a stronger way — an open hexagonal form which takes up more space.

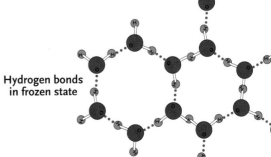

Hydrogen bonds in frozen state

Pure Water Freezes First

Ice lanterns often have white lines or bubbles that reflect the light in beautiful ways.

Why? As water molecules freeze, they line up in tight formation. So tight, in fact, that no other molecules fit. The pure water freezes first, pushing minerals and gases into the warmer center.

If the temperature is cold (around 0°F), water freezes so fast that gases and minerals within can't move out of the way. They become incorporated in the ice, creating lines of tiny bubbles.

If the temperature is just below freezing (15°F to 32°F), water will take longer to freeze and the extra gases and debris will have plenty of time to move away from the cold, making the ice clearer.

The takeaway: If you like clear ice, aim for warmer freezing temps. If you want to experiment with lines and bubbles in the ice, look for colder temps.

— *Photo by Natasha D'Schommer*

Water Freezes from the Outside In

The water inside an uncovered bucket sitting on an insulating surface (frozen ground, snow or Styrofoam) and exposed to be-low-freezing temps, will freeze in the following order:

1. The water on top, where it's in direct contact with the cold air.
2. The water just inside the walls of the container.
3. The water in the center.
4. The water at the bottom of the container.

Why? As discussed on page 8, the hydrogen bonding of water as it freezes (open hex formation) causes ice to expand and become less dense. This is why ice floats rather than sinks — and why it's possible to make ice lanterns, which are just hollow shells of ice.

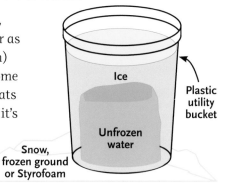

Rate of Freezing Affects Clarity

As we've learned, pure water freezes first, and impurities — like microscopic minerals, dust and even food color — are pushed toward the center where the water is warmer. Most of the impurities therefore are purged when unfrozen water is released to make an ice lantern.

If an ice lantern freezes quickly (-10°F or colder), the impurities can't move toward the center fast enough and may get frozen into the ice. Conversely, if an ice lantern freezes slowly (10°F to 32°F), the impurities have plenty of time to move toward the center so the ice is clearer.

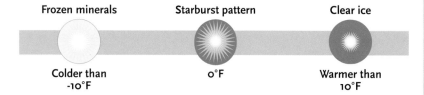

Frozen minerals	Starburst pattern	Clear ice
Colder than -10°F	0°F	Warmer than 10°F

ICE CLARITY

The kind of water used and its temperature will affect the clarity of the ice created.

 Cold tap water has the most air, which will add thrilling ice lines.

 Hot tap water rushes the oxygen out of the water so the ice will be clearer.

 Cold water allowed to freeze slowly (in warmer air temps) permits extra gases and minerals to settle so the ice will be clearer.

 Distilled water still con-tains oxygen that can help create lines, but the ice will be clearer.

 Tap water with a high concentration of minerals and gases will make ice cloudier and even tinted.

 Salted water takes longer to freeze and will make opaque, weak ice.

 Colorants added using the partial-freeze method will mostly drain away with the unfrozen water.

 Using large amounts of food color, Jello, Kool-Aid, or colored sports drinks with the partial-freeze method will help en-hance the ice color. But it's messy — use colored lights instead.

— *Photo by Martha Shull Archer*

Ice Lantern Logic — *Before you begin . . .*

It's worth planning ahead for your first ice lantern.
*Think through the following **5** topics so you'll know what you need.*

#1 Where to Fill?

Basic Water Set-up

For most ice lanterns, all you really need is a sink, bathtub and/or garden hose in an area where you're comfortable working and have easy access to the outdoors or a freezer.

Filling Balloons

To fill heavyweight balloons, it's helpful to have a faucet head small enough to stretch the balloon opening around it.

Faucet head too big? It may be possible to attach a short garden hose (or a trimmed hose section) to your kitchen sink faucet with a garden hose adapter.

DELUXE SINK SET-UP

Since I make hundreds of ice lanterns every year, my sink set-up is a tad more elaborate:

- A deep laundry tub sink with hot and cold unsoftened water.

- A stable riser that can sit inside my sink so I don't have to hunch over while I work. A flow-through surface that doesn't conduct heat is best. My solution? A catch basin kit.

- A stable, waterproof scale that can handle up to 50 lbs.

- An outlet for power tools. *PLEASE USE CAUTION! Using power tools around water can be dangerous!*

- A 4' length of garden hose attached to the faucet for filling ice lantern balloons and larger forms. Cut the metal fitting off the loose end to make it even easier to fill heavyweight balloons.

- Easy access to the outdoors and to a freezer.

For more information, check out the Ice Wrangler's blog at icewrangler.com.

#2 Tools and Supplies

Essential Tool List

All projects in this book come with a list of needed tools, but the following basic tools are essential for all of them:

- Ice lantern forms of your choice — buckets or balloons
- Warm, waterproof gloves
- Candles and matches or LED lights

Other Helpful Tools:

- Scissors
- Power drill
- Spade bits

- Wide paint scraper or putty knife
- Level
- Hammer or Wonder Bar
- Oscillating saw or Sawzall
- Chisel

Freezing Considerations

Most ice lanterns are frozen shells surrounding an airy interior. That means the lantern's bottom and core should stay unfrozen. So where is the best place to freeze ice lanterns? And on what surface?

Where? For the best results, try to place your water-filled forms:

- Out of the sun. The thaw/ freeze cycle that occurs in direct sunlight can slow the speed of freezing. The expansion/contraction of the ice can weaken the freezing form, causing leakage and ice lantern failure.

- At least 2 ft apart. If they're too close together, they'll insulate each other, causing off-center cavities.

- Away from any heated structures that might slow the freezing process and/or offset the location of the cavity.

WHERE TO FREEZE When using the partial-freeze method, the surface on which you place water-filled forms to freeze can affect the shape of your ice lanterns.

LOCATION OF MOLD	GOOD OUTCOME
On snow	Bottom unfrozen, top frozen
On ground	Bottom unfrozen, top frozen
On Styrofoam, on deck	Bottom unfrozen, top frozen
On Styrofoam, on pavement	Bottom unfrozen, top frozen
On Styrofoam, on stone	Bottom unfrozen, top frozen
On deck, Styrofoam cover	Bottom frozen, top unfrozen
On pavement, Styrofoam cover	Bottom frozen, top unfrozen
On stone, Styrofoam cover	Bottom frozen, top unfrozen
On snow, ground or Styrofoam with Styrofoam cover	Top and bottom unfrozen
Spaced > 12 in apart	Cavity centered
Positioned > 10 ft from house	Cavity centered

LOCATION OF MOLD	BAD OUTCOME
In snow	Bottom and sides unfrozen
On pavement	Bottom frozen
On stone	Bottom frozen
On deck	Bottom frozen
Spaced < 12 in apart	Cavity off-center
Positioned < 10 ft from house	Cavity off-center

All ice logic rules apply to both balloons and buckets.

10-15 ft

#4 Pick an Ice Lantern Form   *Size of container and air temperature will determine freezing time.*

Bucket, Balloon or . . .?

Ice lanterns can be created in containers of all shapes and sizes. Your choices are limited only by your imagination, your physical strength and the availability of a freezing environment. In selecting a container, there are certain considerations to keep in mind.

Container Size

Your ability to carry the form filled with water as well as the finished ice lantern should guide your choice of container. Even if you fill the container outside and don't plan to carry it while filled with water, you might want to move the finished lantern at some point.

Small containers of water freeze fast. A small yogurt container, for example, will take just an hour or two to freeze, so you'll need to check it regularly or it could freeze solid.

Conversely, a large container of water can take several days or a week to freeze. If you want to make giant lanterns, you'll need lasting cold weather or access to a large empty deep freezer.

Hold Water

In general, it's useful to choose a form that can hold water. Yet while I used to imagine that ice lanterns could *only* be created in forms that are watertight, it's actually possible to make them even in forms that aren't. *(See Open-Bottom Ice Lantern, p 35.)*

Container Shape

The container you use must be shaped so that the ice lantern can slide out after sitting in a warm room for a short while. If the opening of the container isn't large enough for the ice lantern to slide out, you'll have to cut it off to free the ice lantern. This is why balloons are so handy. Removal is easy: Just cut them off.

Container Integrity

A glass bottle of liquid will usually break in the freezer, and so will a water-filled container that isn't built to expand and contract. Your container must either be replaceable, elastic or built sturdily enough to withstand the rigors of the freezing process.

BALLOON WISDOM

After years of using balloons to make ice lanterns, I've discovered a few secrets:

- Use pressurized tap water or the balloon will not inflate.

- Filling a latex/rubber balloon with hot water softens the material, making the balloon more likely to sag or pop.

- Air left inside a balloon once it's filled with water will rise, creating a flat surface on the top of the ice lantern.

- A balloon's thickness affects its ability to hold a spherical shape.

- Because it's under pressure, water in a balloon will take longer to freeze than water in an unpressurized container.

- Water-filled balloons left in direct sunlight may pop after several days.

- Water-filled balloons will roll around and/or lose their shape unless supported.

- A water-filled balloon can sometimes break while freezing and, once it has begun to leak, can adhere to the surface on which it's sitting.

- A balloon used to make an ice lantern is not reusable. Once the ice lantern has formed, the balloon must be popped and peeled away from the ice.

HOW LONG TO FREEZE?

There are so many variables involved (size, water temp, day/night freezing, container shape, container thickness and desired ice thickness) that it's hard to prescribe specific freezing times for every kind of ice lantern.

Here's a general guide for freezing at 0°F:

- A 32 oz yogurt container will take 8 hours.
- A Bundt pan filled with water will take 12 hours to freeze solid.
- A balloon filled to soccer ball size will take 24 hours.
- A balloon filled to basketball size will take 30 hours.
- An 8" x 24" PVC pipe (bottom sealed with ice) filled with water will take 12 hours.
- A pool of water will take 8 hours to make ice glass, if freezing at night.

24 HOURS at 0°F

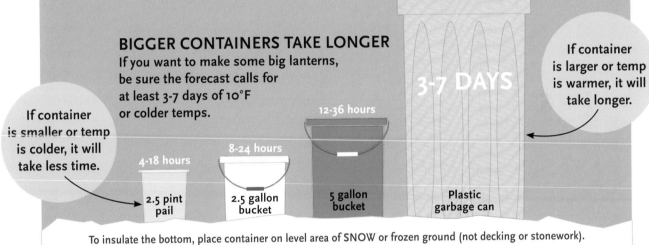

BIGGER CONTAINERS TAKE LONGER

If you want to make some big lanterns, be sure the forecast calls for at least 3-7 days of 10°F or colder temps.

If container is smaller or temp is colder, it will take less time.

If container is larger or temp is warmer, it will take longer.

3-7 DAYS

12-36 hours

8-24 hours

4-18 hours

2.5 pint pail

2.5 gallon bucket

5 gallon bucket

Plastic garbage can

To insulate the bottom, place container on level area of SNOW or frozen ground (not decking or stonework).

#5 Check the Forecast

The Great Outdoor Freezer

If you plan to freeze your ice lanterns outside, you must have weather that is 15°F to 20°F or colder for a minimum of one night or several days. Finished lanterns can survive for a week or more if stored or displayed in temps below 25°F. They'll last even longer if kept out of the sun.

Warm Climate?

Even if you can't count on cold outdoor temps, you can still create ice magic. Just find a level spot in a refrigerator freezer or deep freezer. The size of the freezer will determine the size and quantity of lanterns you can make. Once created, of course, ice lanterns must be stored in a freezer until they're used.

LET'S GET STARTED

You've planned ahead. You've determined your water source. You've gathered your tools and checked the weather forecast. You know where to freeze your lanterns and which forms you want to use. It's time to make some ice lanterns!

PART 2:
Starter Projects

— *Photo by Jennifer Shea Hedberg*

This sun-etched bucket ice lantern was made
with a 7-gallon utility bucket and placed
on a small island in the center of the creek during
the Middlemoon Creekwalk in Minneapolis. .
— Photo by Efrén Solanas
Right: Photo by Bruce Challgren

Partial-Freeze Bucket Ice Lantern

Ice lanterns created in buckets using the partial-freeze method are easy to make, versatile and hold a candle well. The easiest way to explain this process is to imagine a tray of ice cubes taken out of the freezer too soon. What do you find? Crusts of ice with water inside. Release the water and, voilà — miniature ice lanterns. Now we'll do the same thing, but on a much larger scale.

To help illustrate, I made the bucket see-through.

1 FILL

2"

Plastic utility bucket

Water

Snow or Styrofoam

2 FREEZE

Ice

Water

24 HOURS at 0°F

STEP 1: Fill a 5-gallon utility bucket with water about 2" from the top and place it on the snow or frozen ground, making it as level as possible. (Snow and frozen ground will insulate the water in the bottom of the bucket to keep it from freezing.)

STEP 2: Let the water in the bucket freeze overnight. In the morning, look through the exposed ice on the top to see how thick the walls of ice have become. For optimal ice strength, the walls should be 1"-2" thick and there should still be some water left inside.

24 hours at 0°F is a good baseline for allowing the ice lantern's walls to reach ideal thickness. On really cold nights (-10°F to -20°F) it could take as few as 8 hours. At warmer (10°F to 20°F) temps, the process could take up to 36 hours.

TIP

NO COLD WEATHER?
Use a smaller bucket or put it in a deep freezer. Adjust the length of freezing time based on bucket size and temperature (see p 15).

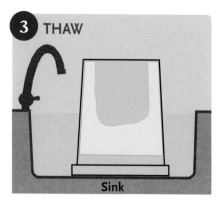

3 THAW

STEP 3: Carry the bucket with ice inside and place upside down in a sink or bathtub to thaw for about 15-30 minutes.

The ice lantern will release from the bucket and slide into the sink. (A towel in a plastic bag under the bucket will lessen the impact on the sink and ice.) Then lift the bucket off the ice.

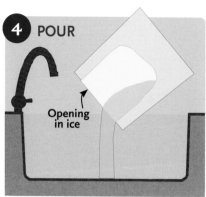

4 POUR

Opening in ice

STEP 4: The upside-down lantern will be filled with water with an opening in the ice on the top. (If not, this will be the weakest part of the ice and can be chipped open using a knife or screwdriver.) Pour the water out of the ice lantern.

5 KEEP FROZEN

STEP 5: Place the lantern on or in a plastic bag in below-freezing temps (outside or freezer) until ready to display.

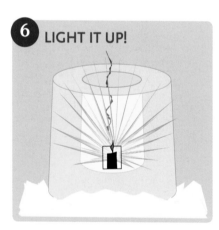

6 LIGHT IT UP!

STEP 6: When you're ready to display the ice lantern, position it with the opening facing up. Place a candle in the bottom of the lantern. Light and enjoy the glow.

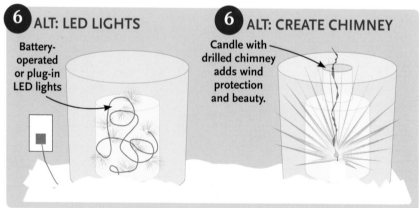

6 ALT: LED LIGHTS

Battery-operated or plug-in LED lights

ALT STEP 6: Fill the cavity of the shell of ice with a string of LED lights made for outdoor use. Place the ice lantern (opening down) on the ground in the desired location and turn on the lights. So easy!

6 ALT: CREATE CHIMNEY

Candle with drilled chimney adds wind protection and beauty.

ALT STEP 6: The magic of a candle, the beauty of the ice and better wind protection make this a great alternative. One extra step is required to create a chimney, but it's well worth the work (*see p 54*).

EXPERIMENT • To Cover or Not to Cover?

WHAT YOU NEED

2 heavy-duty utility buckets and a bucket lid

Cold tap water

Cold temps or deep freezer

Purpose: To demonstrate that covering a bucket while it's freezing will produce an ice lantern with a deep internal cavity.

What to do: Fill two buckets with tap water. Add a bucket lid to one of the buckets and leave the other uncovered. Freeze both using the partial-freeze bucket ice lantern instructions.

Finding: The bucket without the lid will form thick ice on the top, creating a shallow central cavity. The covered bucket will form thin top ice and create a deeper cavity — almost a tube of ice.

Why? The water at the top of the bucket without a lid is exposed to the cold air, so it freezes first and continues freezing until you release the ice, making that area the thickest. In the lid-covered bucket, the water on the sides of the bucket freezes first, then the insulated top, then the middle and finally the bottom which, if sitting in snow or on Styrofoam, will freeze last.

Why is this helpful? If you create a lantern with a larger cavity, the wind will be less likely to blow out your candle.

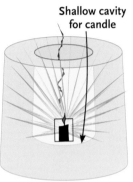
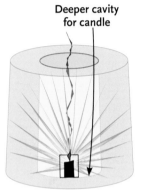

Shallow cavity for candle   Deeper cavity for candle

Bucket without a lid   **Bucket with a lid**

EXPERIMENT • Water Quality = Clarity

WHAT YOU NEED

Several small and replaceable plastic containers

Cold tap water

Cold temps or deep freezer

Purpose: To determine which type of water to use in your ice lanterns, since different water sources freeze with different patterns and clarities.

What to do: Fill a plastic container with cold water from your kitchen tap. Fill another container with water from your laundry and/or garden tap (outside). Finally, fill yet another container with hot distilled water. Label the containers and allow them to freeze solid.

Finding: Analyze the ice inside each container. The ice that looks best to you indicates the water type you should use to fill your ice lantern containers.

Why is this helpful? Many homes soften their water. Water that is softened (with added salt) will make ice that is weak and opaque. Water from a laundry or garden tap is rarely softened and therefore preferable for making ice lanterns. Distilled/hot water creates clearer ice lanterns.

Clearer ice   Star pattern ice   Opaque ice

Frozen distilled hot water   **Frozen plain tap water**   **Frozen softened tap water**

An ice lantern made using the freeze-solid method is often cloudy because minerals and gases in the water are frozen into the ice.
— *Photo by Jennifer Shea Hedberg*

✳ Freeze-Solid Bucket Ice Lantern

With this freeze-solid set-up, you can fill the buckets, put them in the freezer or outside, and quite literally forget them. I have seen many methods for making freeze-solid bucket ice lanterns that involve weights, tape, and other techniques. While they work fine, I find my set-up is virtually foolproof. The center cavity is created by using a smaller bucket inside a larger bucket. The size of the smaller bucket determines the size of the interior cavity where the candle or LED lights will be placed.

An added benefit of this method is that adding food color to the ice will be much more successful because the water freezes solid. The negative to this method is that the extra minerals and gases in the water will be frozen into the ice, so unless you use absolutely pure water, the ice will become cloudy and weak.

WHAT YOU NEED

2-gallon utility bucket with snap-on lid

1-quart utility bucket with snap-on lid

1 • .25" x 1" galvanized carriage bolt

2 • .25" galvanized washers

1 • .25" galvanized wing nut

Cold tap water

Cold temps or deep freezer

Candle in candle holder

Matches

To help illustrate, I made the large bucket see-through.

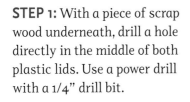

1 DRILL LIDS

Large bucket lid center ↲

Small bucket lid center ↰

STEP 1: With a piece of scrap wood underneath, drill a hole directly in the middle of both plastic lids. Use a power drill with a 1/4" drill bit.

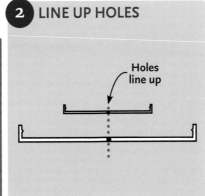

2 LINE UP HOLES

Holes line up ↓

STEP 2: Place the two lids together with the holes lining up. The inside of both lids should face up.

③ SECURE LIDS

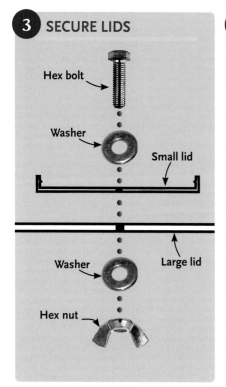

Hex bolt

Washer

Small lid

Washer

Large lid

Hex nut

④ SNAP IN SMALL LID

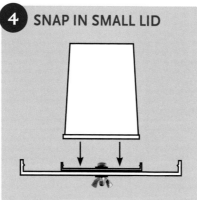

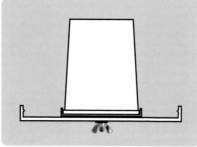

STEP 4: Snap the empty small plastic bucket into the small lid.

⑤ FILL

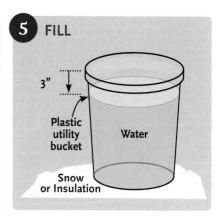

3"

Plastic utility bucket

Water

Snow or Insulation

STEP 5: Fill a 2-gallon utility bucket with water approximately 3" from top.

STEP 3: Thread the bolt with one washer and put through the bottom of the small lid and out the hole in the large lid. Place the second washer on the bolt followed by the winged hex nut and tighten.

TIP

HOW MUCH WATER?
To determine the actual amount of water needed to fill the large bucket before adding the small bucket, first fill the large bucket to 1" from the top with water.

Then take the small bucket and fill it with water from the big bucket. (This should be the amount of water that will be displaced by the small bucket.)

Empty the water from the small bucket into the sink and snap the empty small bucket into its lid.

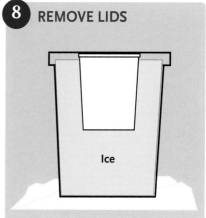

6 ADD BIG LID

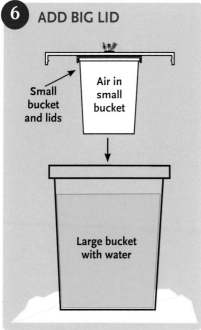

Small bucket and lids

Air in small bucket

Large bucket with water

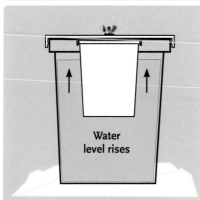

Water level rises

STEP 6: Lower the combined lids and small bucket into the water in the large bucket. Snap the large lid onto the large bucket.

Note: Be prepared for the small bucket to displace water from the lower bucket.

7 FREEZE SOLID

Ice

STEP 7: Put the combined buckets in below-freezing temps on any surface you like. (It will freeze solid, so the surface does not matter.) Allow the water to freeze for at least 24 hours or until all the water has frozen.

8 REMOVE LIDS

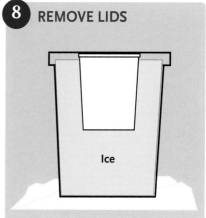

Ice

STEP 8: Once the water has frozen solid, unscrew the wing nut and remove both of the plastic lids and all hardware pieces. The small bucket will be frozen into the ice.

24 HOURS at 0°F

12 1 2 3 4 5 6 7 8 9 10 11

9 ADD WATER

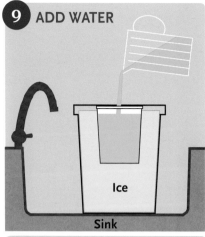

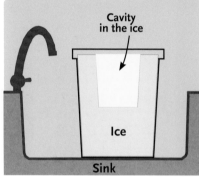

STEP 9: Put the buckets in a sink and fill the small bucket with warm water. Allow it to sit for a few minutes until the small bucket slips free. There is now a cavity in the ice.

10 THAW

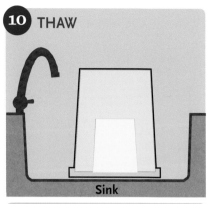

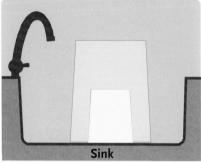

STEP 10: Flip the large bucket upside down in the sink and let it sit for a few minutes until the ice slips free.

Put the lantern in a plastic bag and keep in freezing temps until ready to use.

11 LIGHT

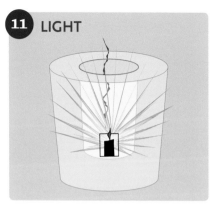

STEP 11: When you're ready to use the ice lantern, arrange it with the opening facing up and place a candle in the bottom of the cavity. Light and enjoy.

See lighting alternatives below.

Flip over the lantern and fill the cavity with plug-in or battery-operated LED lights.

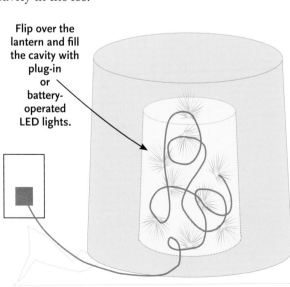

For windy conditions, consider flipping the ice lantern over and drilling a chimney with a power drill (see p 55).

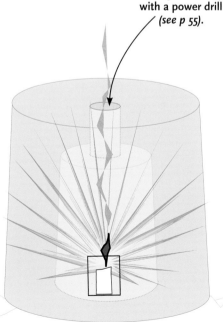

Equipment to make
one partial-freeze
bucket ice lantern with
2-gallon utility bucket
(See p 19)

Equipment to make
one freeze-solid
bucket ice lantern with
2-gallon utility bucket
(See p 23)

Liquid food color

Purpose: To determine which ice lantern-making method works best to color the ice with food color, Jello, Kool-Aid, colored sports drinks, etc.

What to do:

1. Fill two 2-gallon utility buckets with cold tap water to 1" below top of bucket.

2. Use the quart container to remove one full quart of water from one of the buckets.

3. Add 80 drops of food color to each bucket of water and stir until color is blended. (*Tip:* For better comparison, add the same amount and color to each bucket.)

4. Add the bucket lid with the small bucket attached as per directions on page 24, and snap onto the top of the bucket with less water.

5. Freeze the bucket without the lid according to the partial-freeze method.

6. Freeze the bucket with the lid according to the freeze-solid method.

7. Remove the ice from both buckets and compare color differences.

Finding: The bucket ice lantern made with the freeze-solid method will be more vibrantly colored than the bucket ice lantern made with the partial-freeze method.

Why is this helpful? Pure water freezes first. Impurities, like food color, are pushed toward the center of the bucket where it's warmer. When using the partial-freeze method, the freezing process is stopped before the water becomes solid and the water in the center is released to form a cavity. Because the colorant is an impurity, most of it will be released with the unfrozen water. The resulting ice lantern will be faintly colored. If more colorant is used or sugar/salt are combined with the colorant, the ice color may intensify.

When colorants are added using the freeze-solid method, the ice will be highly colored but could crack or weaken as it expands. ***Warning! Food color can stain skin, wood, cloth and other porous surfaces.***

Partial-freeze method   **Freeze-solid method**

Globe Ice Lantern
(using partial-freeze method)

Many people think that a globe ice lantern, made in an industrial-strength balloon, is the most modern of ice lantern shapes. But perhaps the very first ice lantern was made by an ancient human who froze a sheep's bladder full of water to protect a fragile flame on a cold winter night. I like to think it could be true.

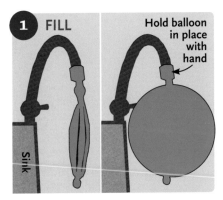

1 FILL

Hold balloon in place with hand

Sink

STEP 1: Fill a globe ice lantern balloon with cold tap water by stretching the balloon's mouth around the water faucet head to form a seal. Hold the balloon tightly in place with thumb and forefinger as the pressurized water from the tap fills it to the desired size.

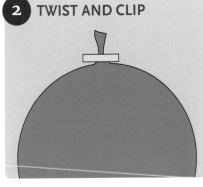

2 TWIST AND CLIP

STEP 2: Twist the neck of the balloon and seal it with an easy-close balloon clip (available in Wintercraft® Globe Ice Lantern Kits) or tie it closed.

TIP

RELEASE EXTRA AIR
Before you close the balloon, open the top slightly to let the air escape that has risen to the top.

Why? When you fill a balloon with water, air will be forced inside with it. If you don't release the air, it will stay at the top of the balloon while it freezes, causing the globe ice lantern to have a flat top. (See *Ice Person Lantern, p 165.*)

Left: This stunning globe ice lantern is lit with a candle and shines brilliantly against several sheets of ice glass.

Right: Globe ice lanterns light up a restaurant entrance for an event.
— *Photos by Jennifer Shea Hedberg*

③ FREEZING BASE

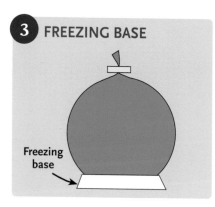

Freezing
base

④ FREEZE OUTSIDE

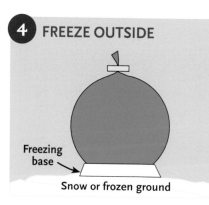

Freezing
base

Snow or frozen ground

FREEZE IN FREEZER

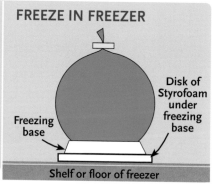

Freezing
base

Disk of
Styrofoam
under
freezing
base

Shelf or floor of freezer

STEP 3: To help the balloon keep a nice round shape while it freezes, place it in a steady base. The round waterproof dish found in the Wintercraft® Globe Ice Lantern Kit works well. Alternatives include a low dog dish, pie pan or plastic plant saucer.

STEP 4: Freeze the filled balloon outside in a mostly shaded area (best if average temperature is below 15°F). Place the balloon and freezing base directly on the ground or snow to keep the bottom of the ice globe from freezing.

ALT STEP 4: Freeze the filled balloon in a freezer with the freezing base on a piece of Styrofoam, which will simulate the insulating effect of snow/ground. This will help keep the ice lantern bottom from freezing.

24 HOURS at 0°F

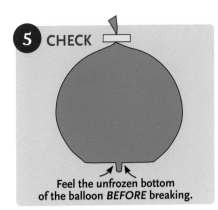

⑤ CHECK

Feel the unfrozen bottom of the balloon *BEFORE* breaking.

⑥ PEEL AND RELEASE

⑦ LIGHT AND ENJOY!

STEP 5: Give the water time to freeze, then check to see if a shell of ice has formed by pushing firmly on the balloon while it sits in the freezing base.

If your balloon sits nicely on a 6" freezing base, wait and check after 14-18 hours.

If your balloon sits nicely on an 8" freezing base, wait and check after 24-30 hours.

When a shell of ice forms, lift the balloon off its base and feel the unfrozen bottom.

If the bottom is completely unfrozen, the shell of ice will be thin (.25"-.5"). If more thickness is desired (1"-3"), continue freezing and recheck in 6-8 hours.

If the bottom is slushy or feels like it's closing up, the shell of ice will be thicker (1"-3").

Ice thickness varies with freezing time, volume of water and temperature. Experiment and have fun!

Left: Photo by Martha Shull Archer

STEP 6: When the shell of ice has reached the desired thickness, slice open the balloon using a pair of scissors or a sharp knife and peel it from the ice. The water that didn't freeze will come gushing out of the open bottom.

STEP 7: Place the shell of ice with the opening facing up on the ground in the desired location. Place a floating candle inside and light with a match.

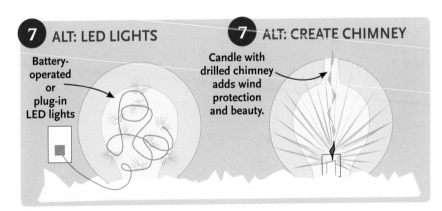

⑦ ALT: LED LIGHTS

Battery-operated or plug-in LED lights

⑦ ALT: CREATE CHIMNEY

Candle with drilled chimney adds wind protection and beauty.

ALT STEP 7: Fill the cavity of the shell of ice with a string of LED lights appropriate for outdoor use. Place the ice lantern and lights on the ground with the opening facing down and turn on the lights.

ALT STEP 7: Place the lantern's opening over the candle. More steps are required to create a chimney and adjust air flow *(see p 54)*, but the result is well worth the effort. The magic of a candle, the beauty of the ice and better wind protection make this alternative the best.

WHAT YOU NEED

Several
ice lantern balloons

Food color

Tap water

Cold temps

Purpose: To judge the effect that adding salt and colorant to water has on an ice lantern's clarity and color. Using colorant with the partial-freeze method rarely produces a highly colored ice lantern: Most of the colorant escapes with the unfrozen water. How does adding salt impact color intensity?

What to do: Label the balloons according to the amounts of salt and food color you will use. Add specified amounts of salt and food color to the unfilled balloons. Fill the balloons with equal amounts of tap water and set them in cold temps to freeze. This set froze for 19 hours (10am-5am) at 0°F.

Finding: Increasing amounts of salt will make the finished ice more opaque and cause the color to intensify. More effective colorants are Jello mixes, colored sports drinks and Kool-Aid because all contain high levels of salt.

	No salt (NaCl)	.25 tsp/1ml salt (NaCl)	.5 tsp/2ml salt (NaCl)
0 drops food color			
20 drops food color			
40 drops food color			
60 drops food color			

Warning! Food color can stain skin, wood, cloth and other porous surfaces.

EXPERIMENT • "Kissing Lanterns"

WHAT YOU NEED

4 ice lantern balloons

Cold tap water

Cold temps or deep freezer

Purpose: To demonstrate that an ice lantern will freeze from the outside in — or, to put it another way, the coldest water will freeze first.

What to do: Fill 4 balloons with water and place them in below-freezing temps. Position 2 of the balloons so they're very close or "kissing." Place the other 2 balloons at least 2 ft apart from each other. (If outside, place all balloons away from buildings, the heat of which could interfere with the experiment.)

Conclusion: The balloons placed close together will create globe ice lanterns with off-center cavities and perhaps with holes in the sides of the ice — not desirable! The ice lanterns made by the two balloons placed farther apart will have centered cavities and evenly thick sides.

Why? When two balloons are put next to each other, the water just inside the balloons (where they are close) is kept warm — making that area the second warmest spot in each balloon. The water at the bottom of the balloons, if it's sitting in snow or on a piece of Styrofoam, will be the warmest.

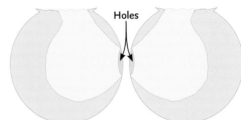

Holes

Globe ice lanterns with holes in their sides

EXPERIMENT • Balloon Thickness Study

WHAT YOU NEED

Different types of balloons

Cold/hot tap water

Purpose: To determine the flexibility differences between balloon types.

What to do: Fill a variety of balloons with the same amount of cold and hot water. Observe differences in flexibility when the water temperature changes. Note which balloon types stretch or "blob" and which hold their shape.

Conclusion: Heavyweight balloons filled with cold water will stretch the least. Thin party balloons filled with warm water will stretch the most.

Why is this helpful?

It's worthwhile to understand which balloon is right for creating each kind of ice lantern. Example: Bargain punching balls are best for making the *Teardrop Ice Lantern (see p 83)* since they stretch with warm water but can also withstand the rigors of hanging.

Optional: a freezing base, or other support for the balloon, will help the balloon retain a rounder shape with cold water applications.

Heavyweight punching ball cold water

Lightweight punching ball cold water

24" Party balloon cold water

11" Party balloon cold water

Heavyweight punching ball warm water

Lightweight punching ball warm water

24" Party balloon warm water

11" Party balloon warm water

TIP

SELECTING THE PIPE?
PVC pipes in home improvement stores are precut — some will be cut straighter than others. Pull a few out and stand them on their ends. Pick the one that stands the straightest.

Open-Bottom Ice Lantern
(using partial-freeze method)

Ice can be used to seal the bottom of any form that normally does not hold water — a PVC pipe, for instance. Once one of the ends is sealed with ice, the mold can be filled with water and frozen just like any other bucket. The amazing thing about this process is that it can be applied to many different non-watertight forms made of waterproof material.

To help illustrate, I made the PVC pipe see-through.

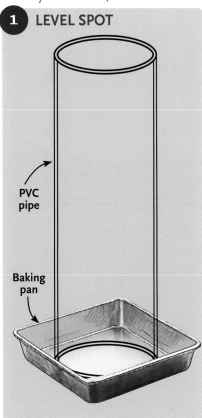

1 LEVEL SPOT

PVC pipe

Baking pan

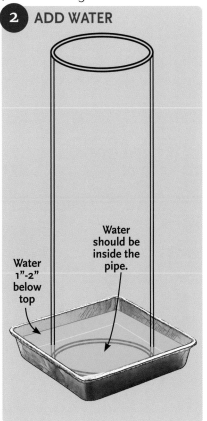

2 ADD WATER

Water should be inside the pipe.

Water 1"-2" below top

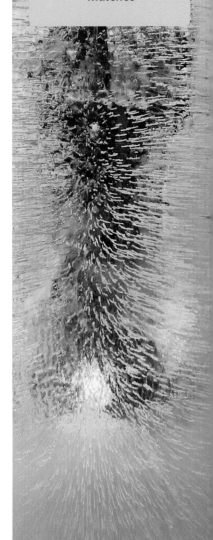

STEP 1: Place the baking pan on the flat bottom of a deep freezer or a level stone or wood surface in below-freezing temps. Stand the PVC pipe on its straightest end inside the baking pan.

STEP 2: Fill the baking pan with water up to .5"-1" below the top edge. The water should be inside and outside the pipe.

3 FREEZE SOLID

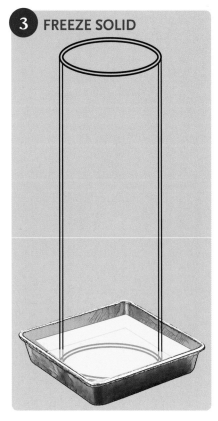

STEP 3: Allow the water in the pan and in the PVC pipe to freeze solid. Depending on the temperature, this could take several hours.

4 ADD WATER

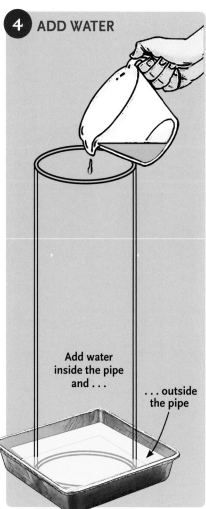

Add water inside the pipe and . . .

. . . outside the pipe

STEP 4: Add 1/2 cup water inside the PVC pipe and 1/2 cup water outside the PVC pipe and let that water freeze for at least an hour.

Why? When water is allowed to freeze solid, it can break under the pressure. This small amount of water will fill any gaps that might develop.

5 FILL

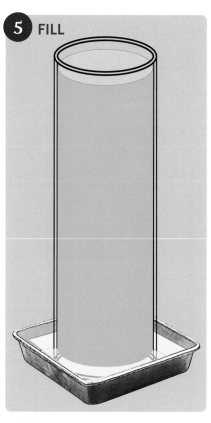

STEP 5: Now that the bottom has been sealed with ice, the PVC pipe can be filled with water to within 1"-2" from the top.

TIP

LEAKING

When adding water to the PVC pipe (after the bottom has been sealed with ice), water leakage is still a possibility. Consider first adding 2-3 cups of CHILLED water inside the PVC pipe. Let it sit for 10 minutes and check that no water emerges outside the pipe before filling the PVC pipe with water.

6 ADD TOP AND FREEZE

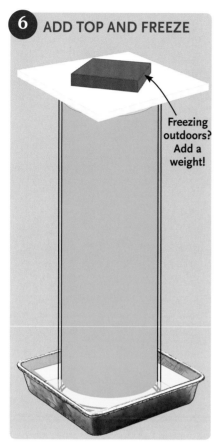

Freezing outdoors? Add a weight!

7 EMPTY AND THAW

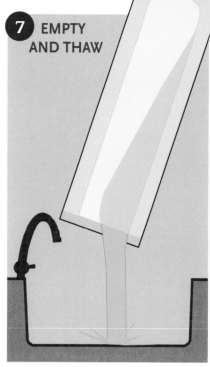

8 REMOVE EXTRA ICE

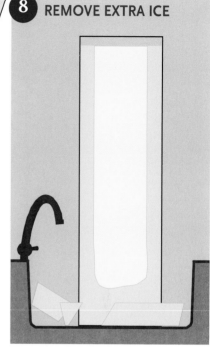

STEP 6: Cover the top with a piece of Styrofoam (or anything that will insulate the opening of the PVC pipe). If outside, weigh down the top with a rock or brick to keep it from blowing away.

Let the water in the pipe freeze for 12 hours. Lift the Styrofoam to check for ice thickness periodically. *Do not freeze solid!*

Why use Styrofoam? The bottom of the PVC pipe is sealed with ice and the top of the ice cylinder must remain open to allow the unfrozen water to be easily released.

STEP 7: When the ice cylinder has frozen with a center cavity of at least 3", turn the PVC pipe upside down in a sink and let the water that did not freeze flow out the open top. (If the top isn't open, create a hole with a drill or ice pick to release the water.)

STEP 8: Place the PVC pipe with the ice inside right side up in a sink or bathtub to thaw for 15-30 minutes.

Remove the baking pan and gently break off the ice outside of the PVC pipe with a hammer, screwdriver or ice pick.

12 HOURS at 0°F

TIP

FREEZING WINDOW
A 6" PVC pipe isn't very big, so the window of opportunity for keeping a hollow chamber in the ice is smaller than you might think. Start with 12 hours in 0°F. If it hasn't frozen enough, continue freezing, but check back once an hour.

9 REMOVE TUBE

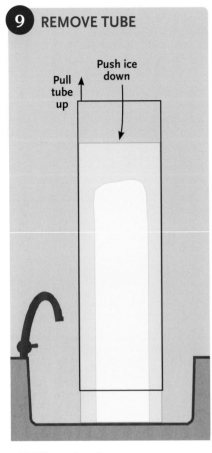

Pull
tube
up

Push ice
down

STEP 9: Flip the PVC pipe upside down and push the ice cylinder down with one hand while lifting the PVC pipe up with your other hand.

TIP

ICE NOT MOVING?
The surface tension between ice and a PVC pipe with straight sides is significant. If it does not come out easily, thaw 15 minutes longer and try again. Laying the PVC pipe on its side and pushing the ice out is another good alternative.

10 LIGHT AND ENJOY

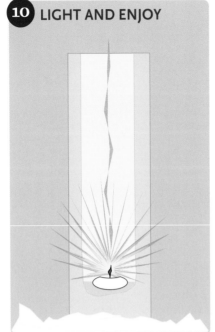

STEP 10: Place the shell of ice with the opening facing up on the ground in the desired location. Place a floating candle inside and light with a match.

TIP

REUSE PVC PIPE
A perk of using high quality PVC pipes to make ice luminaries is that the pipes can be used over and over again.

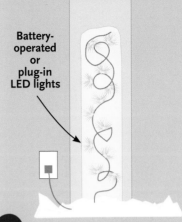

Battery-
operated
or
plug-in
LED lights

10 ALT: LED LIGHTS

Fill the cavity of the shell of ice with a string of LED lights intended for outdoor use. Place the ice lantern and lights on the ground in the desired location and turn on the lights.

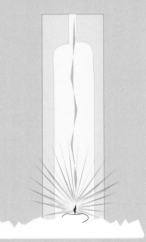

10 ALT: CREATE CHIMNEY

The magic of a candle, the beauty of the ice and excellent wind protection make this alternative the best. Another step is required to create a chimney, but it's well worth it (see p 54).

Think Big!

The creators of the City of Lakes Luminary Loppet in Minneapolis create giant ice cylinder lanterns with the large cardboard tubes used to make cement columns and footings. Round trenches are routed into lake ice to fit the large tubes exactly. The interiors of the large tubes are sealed with a waterproofing material and then placed into the trenches with a small amount of water.

After the bottoms are sealed with ice, the huge tubes are filled with lake water. Once crusts of ice have grown a few inches thick, the cardboard tubes are sliced and peeled off. Holes are drilled into the bottoms of the ice cylinders to release the water. To light the giant ice lanterns, candles are attached to contraptions designed to hang from the top. These towers of ice are amazing and a main visual attraction of the event.

Large cardboard tubes designed to make cement columns are used to create super-sized ice cylinders at the City of Lakes Luminary Loppet, an annual winter event in Minneapolis. — Photo by John Breitinger

Surround Ice Lantern
(Pieces of ice that protect a candle)

Aluminum foil pans, sheet cake pans, shaped cake pans, plastic trays, clear plastic tops of catering trays and even stepping stone molds are just a few of the shallow containers that can be used to create thin shapes of ice. These pieces of ice can then be glued together with snow, water or a mixture of both called "snice" to create a protective shield for a candle or LED lights.

Decorations? I have added an orange slice, a juniper branch and some cranberries to the ice for visual interest. A surround ice lantern can be made with plain ice of any shape or size. The main goal of the ice pieces is to protect the candle from the wind.

What makes these surround ice lanterns so easy is that the ice can be frozen solid, so no timing is necessary. The resulting ice will be somewhat opaque, but that will make the decorations you add stand out visually within the ice.

1 LEVEL SPOT

Aluminum foil pan
or other shallow container

2 ADD WATER

STEP 1: Place an aluminum foil pan on the flat bottom of a deep freezer or a level stone or wood surface outside in below-freezing temps.

STEP 2: Fill the baking pan with about 1"-1.5" of water.

Left: The spring thaw makes snow easily packable to secure this surround ice lantern. — Photo by Jennifer Shea Hedberg

Right: Molds used to create thin pieces of ice. — Photo by Pat Palanuk

WHAT YOU NEED

4 aluminum foil pans

Orange slices

Juniper branches

Cranberries

Distilled or tap water

Cold temps or deep freezer

Candle in candle holder

Matches

3 ADD DECORATIONS

STEP 3: Place the juniper branch in the water, then the orange slice, then the cranberries. All should float. Arrange as your creativity dictates.

4 FREEZE

8 HOURS at 0°F

STEP 4: Let the water freeze solid by leaving the pan for several hours in below-freezing temps. The ice will likely be cloudy/white/translucent toward the bottom of the pan.

5 THAW

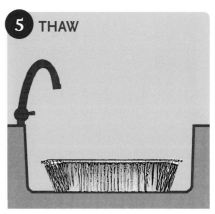

STEP 5: Place the ice-filled pan in a sink to thaw for about 15 minutes.

TIP

OTHER DECORATIONS?

Add more branches, orange slices or other decorations, but keep in mind the following ideas:

- Less is more!
- Items that float will be seen more clearly in the ice.
- Solid items will be silhouetted by the candlelight.
- Colored translucent items will glow with the light.

6 RELEASE ICE

STEP 6: After the ice has thawed, it should slip easily from the pan. Use care, as the ice will be fragile.

7 STORE AND REPEAT

STEP 7: Place the ice in a plastic bag and store in below-freezing temps until all 4 of the ice pieces are created and you're ready to display.

8 DISPLAY WITH SNOW

9 ADD ICE

10 ADD MORE ICE

STEP 8: Make sure there is at least one shovelful of packable snow in the spot where you want to display your ice lantern.

Place one piece of ice so it stands straight.

STEP 9: Add another panel of ice at a 90° angle to the first panel. Arrange to minimize gaps between the ice pieces.

STEP 10: Add the third piece of ice, as before.

TIP

MAKE "SNICE"
When it's too cold for packable snow, make "snice" — a mixture of snow and water. Fill a bucket half full with water, then add snow. Mix and add more snow and/or more water until it feels like thin paste. Use it to "glue" the pieces into place. It's also a great way to fill any gaps in the ice where the wind could blow through. *Be sure to wear waterproof gloves (see p 8).*

11 ADD FINAL PIECE

12 ADD LIGHT

STEP 11: Add the final piece of ice and check for gaps between the ice pieces. Fill the gaps with packable snow or snice.

STEP 12: Place a candle in the center of the ice pieces and light. *Optional:* Turn on a battery-operated LED light and place it in the center of the ice pieces.

Shards of lake ice pile up
on the shores of Lake Superior near
Duluth, Minnesota. The sun shines
through them and makes for
a dazzling natural display.
— Photo by Tom Hedberg

Right: Sunlit ice glass
— Photo by Martha Shull Archer

Ice Glass

I make these vertical sheets of organically shaped ice in pools in my front yard and use them with ice lanterns to reflect their light up into the air.

I started making ice glass after a trip up north to Lake Superior where I saw huge shards of ice thrown up on the shore at every angle. The sunlight passed through them and, wham, I thought, I can make that!

After several attempts, I found a way. With snow for shaping and plastic sheeting for a non-porous layer, I created a pool and filled it with water. The bottom of the pool was heated by the earth and the water surface was exposed to the cold, so a layer of ice formed on top. When the layer was 1.5"-2" thick, I pulled it from the pool and left the rest of the water in the pool to freeze into a new layer. I repeated the process until there was no water left in the pool. Each layer was different. Pure water freezes first, so the "first pull" was very clear and flat. The "second pull" was more mineral-rich and thus more translucent, and the pool's bottom started to make impressions in the ice. The "final pull" was opaque and produced ice with wild convolutions on the surface.

Let's get started on your ice glass pool . . .

To help illustrate, I made the balloons pink
and the plastic sheeting light green and see-through.

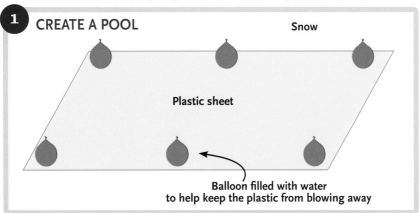

1 CREATE A POOL

Snow

Plastic sheet

Balloon filled with water
to help keep the plastic from blowing away

STEP 1: In a relatively flat snow-covered area, lay out a piece of plastic sheeting and put a water balloon at each corner and in the middle of the two longer sides to keep the plastic from blowing away.

WHAT YOU NEED

Snow

Snow shovel

9'x12' plastic sheeting
(never been used)

6 water balloons
filled with water
(clipped or tied closed)

Garden hose

Gloves
(waterproof and warm)

Any ice lantern

Candle
in candle holder

Matches

② BARRIER WALLS

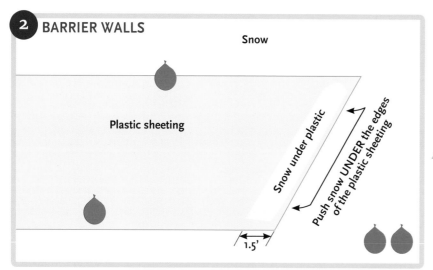

STEP 2: Barrier walls of snow must be made under the plastic and then secured again with the water-filled balloons. Start with one end and work your way around. Take two balloons off and push snow under the plastic about 1.5' so that the plastic comes down on the outside enough to be secured with the balloon. Try to make the wall of snow at least 6"-10" high. Continue pushing snow under the plastic to form 4 walls. Secure with water-filled balloons and reinforce with more snow if available.

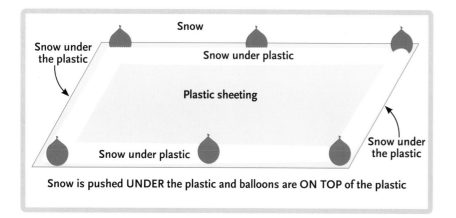

Snow is pushed UNDER the plastic and balloons are ON TOP of the plastic

③ ADD WATER

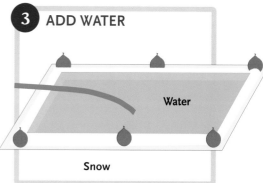

STEP 3: Hook up the garden hose and put one end in the middle of the plastic sheeting. Turn on the water and fill up the pool. My ice glass pools are approximately 4' x 8' and around 5"-6" deep.

TIP

WARNING! While filling the pool with water, if you notice water leaking from a hole in the plastic, lift up the plastic and add some snow underneath the hole. When you lay the plastic back down, the hole should be in the middle of a raised island in the pool of water. Likewise, if there is a weak portion of the snow wall, lift the plastic sheeting up and push more snow under the plastic in areas where water is escaping.

NO HOSE? Fill 5-gallon utility buckets with water and bring to the pools. Ask a few friends to help organize a bucket brigade!

4 FREEZE

Ice

8 HOURS at **0°F**

STEP 4: Let the water freeze until the top of the pool has formed a crust of ice approximately 1.5"–2" thick.

To determine the thickness of the crust of ice, push the plastic into the snow underneath and away from the ice to create a hollow space to get a finger or two under the ice. Pinch the ice between your fingers. How thick does it feel? If thin, let it freeze longer. If just right, proceed to next step.

Do NOT let pools of water freeze solid!

5 PULL OUT ICE

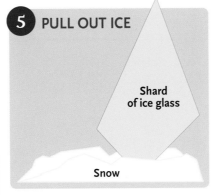

Shard of ice glass

Snow

STEP 5: When the ice is sufficiently thick, it's ready to harvest.

Create piles of snow near the pool where the harvested ice will be stored until ready to use.

To harvest the ice glass, work at the pool's edge to get a few fingers under the ice surface. With two handholds, gently lift the ice up until it naturally breaks and a piece becomes separate. Remove the ice from the pool. *Don't pierce the plastic with a pointy end of ice or the plastic will start to leak.* Put the piece of ice vertically into a pile of snow to store it.

TIP

DON'T WORRY
The magic of ice glass is its unplanned variation — the beautiful, organic nature of each piece — so enjoy the imperfection!

6 ALL OUT

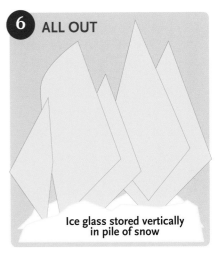

Ice glass stored vertically in pile of snow

STEP 6: Continue pulling out all the ice that has formed and store the ice glass vertically in piles of snow until ready to use.

7 FREEZE AGAIN

Ice

6 HOURS at **0°F**

STEP 7: Let the remaining water in the pool freeze again until there's a new crust of ice. Harvest that ice. Repeat Steps 4-6 until there is no water left in the pool. Freezing time will shorten with each batch of ice glass as the pool's depth diminishes.

Note: The first pull of ice is clear, but each time the pool refreezes, the ice becomes more mineral-rich and opaque.

8 START BUILDING WITH LIGHT

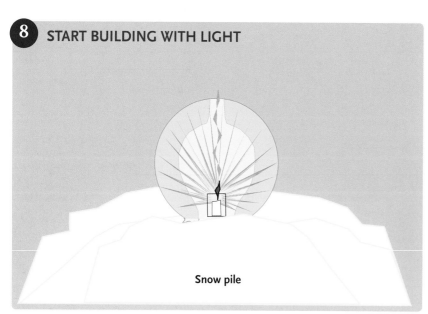

Snow pile

STEP 8: Place an ice lantern in the middle of a large pile of snow. Either light the candle of the ice lantern now, or make sure to leave access through the added ice glass to light it later.

9 CHOOSE ICE

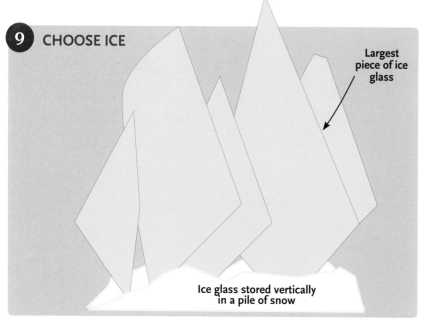

Largest piece of ice glass

Ice glass stored vertically in a pile of snow

STEP 9: Select the largest piece of ice glass from your collection and loosen it from the snow.

10 LOOSEN ICE

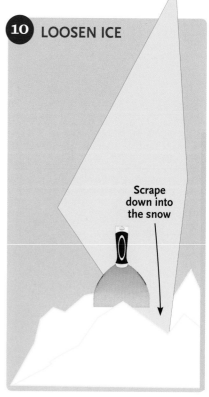

Scrape down into the snow

STEP 10: To loosen a piece of ice glass from a pile of snow, hold the ice glass with one hand and scrape a large paint scraper against the ice and into the snow with your other hand. Scrape both sides of the ice glass. Don't push against the ice glass, but rock each piece from side to side to loosen.

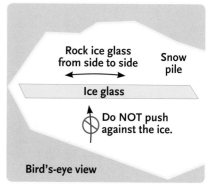

Rock ice glass from side to side

Snow pile

Ice glass

Do NOT push against the ice.

Bird's-eye view

11 ICE GLASS IN SNOW

When positioning ice glass, be careful not to disturb the ice lantern or its air flow.

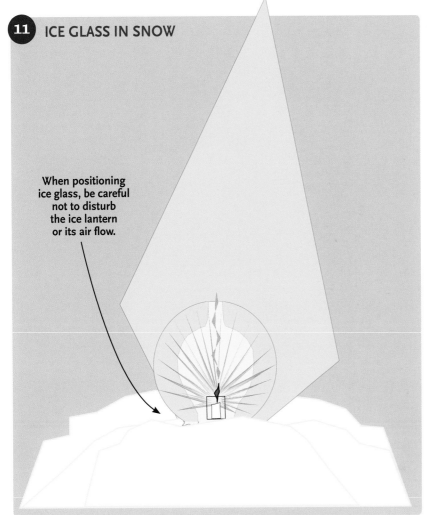

12 MORE ICE

STEP 12: Continue adding pieces of ice glass around the ice lantern — both behind it . . .

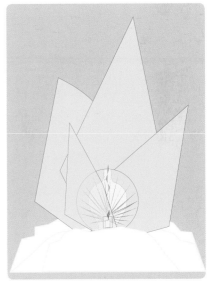

STEP 11: Place the piece of ice glass into the snow behind the ice lantern, but try not to disturb the lantern's air flow or stability. Add extra snow near the base of the ice glass to make sure it stays up. In warmer temps (15°F to 32°F) it's easy to pack snow around the base of the ice glass to secure it, but given how long it takes to freeze into position, it's wise to keep the ice vertical. When temps are colder (below 15°F), the ice will freeze faster into the snow, so the ice glass can be arranged at more extreme angles. Experiment with placement to see how the light bounces off the ice edges.

. . . and in front. Each piece will reflect the light differently. The trick is to know when to stop adding ice. When in doubt, just add another ice lantern and keep going!

PART 3: Display Logic

Extra-large globe ice lanterns light up the walkway to a festive holiday party.
— Photo by Jennifer Shea Hedberg

Displaying Ice Luminaries — *Guidelines and Tips*

Whether you're looking for ways to show off freshly made ice lanterns or preparing to make luminaries to fit a display plan you already have in mind, here are a few things you'll want to consider:

- ❖ *Candle vs. LED Lights vs. Sunlight*
- ❖ *Indoor vs. Outdoor*
- ❖ *Composition*
- ❖ *Finishing Touches*

Your choices for illuminating the ice lanterns will determine the display's mood, the color of its light and whether convenience will rule the day. LED lights offer bright, colorful light with relative ease, but a flame flickering inside ice is simply magical. You get to make the choice.

LET'S START with CANDLES *An average candle will burn brightest and stay lit with a sufficient and shielded air supply. To achieve this, an ice lantern needs a chimney so the heated air can escape. Here are two methods for creating chimneys.*

#1 Quick Flip Chimney

By design, an ice lantern is made by insulating one end so that it stays unfrozen. If positioned upward, this opening becomes the chimney. Pop a lit candle inside and you're done.

Benefits:
Fast and easy!

Cons:

Candle may go out in the wind.
Because the opening is large, the candle is vulnerable to wind.

Candle can drown.
A flipped ice lantern is a bowl of ice with a candle inside. As the candle burns, the bowl fills with melted ice, and a standard candle will eventually drown.

Not good indoors.
Warm indoor temps make ice melt quickly, so a regular candle will drown faster.

Drowning Candle Options:

Let the water escape.
Drilling a small hole in the side near the bottom of the ice lantern will allow water to drip out. The hole also lets air in to feed the candle.

Use floating candles.
Floating candles rise with the water. The drawback: As the water rises, so does the candle — nearer to the wind, which can extinguish the flame.

Drilled hole allows melting ice to drain away and lets air in to feed the candle.

Bucket ice lantern

Use floating candles with the quick flip method.

Teardrop ice lantern

Globe ice lantern

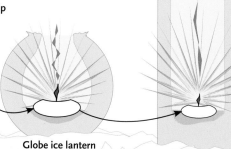

Open-bottom ice lantern

A teardrop ice lantern hangs in a tree,
suspended by a fish line macramé pot holder.
A hole drilled in the side toward the bottom
allows melting ice to drip away.
— Photo by Stephen L. Garrett

#2 Drilled Chimney

Another way to create an ice lantern chimney is to drill a small hole in the frozen end of the lantern. With this method, the large opening in the ice faces down.

There are two ways to drill a chimney (*see diagrams next page*). You can let the candle's heat drill the hole, or use a power drill and a spade bit.

Benefits:

More attractive. The most beautiful side of the ice lantern faces up where it can be seen.

Stable. The flat side of the ice lantern faces down.

Wind protection. The candle is less likely to be extinguished.

Illumination. A candle placed low to the ground lights up the entire lantern.

Versatility. Because the open bottom allows the melting ice to escape, the lantern can be used indoors.

Con:

Air flow concerns. Without a secondary air passageway, the lantern's candle will struggle for air and suffocate.

This globe ice lantern has a chimney created with a power drill and spade bit. While this type of chimney requires extra effort, it's best for high wind situations and enhanced beauty. — Photo by Todd Buchanan

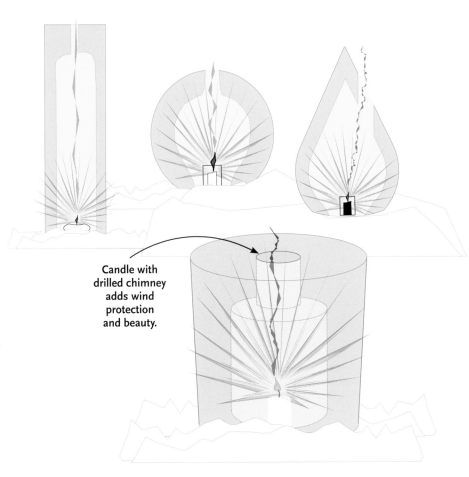

Candle with drilled chimney adds wind protection and beauty.

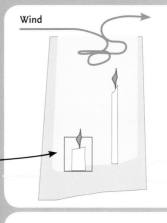

USING CANDLES IN THE WIND

If the candle flame inside your ice lantern dances wildly or goes out, you have too much wind for a quick flip chimney. Here are three high-wind solutions:

#1: LOWER THE CANDLE

A tall taper candle burning in a bucket lantern can be elegant, but it's impractical in high-wind conditions. I commonly use a short 10-hour votive candle in a candle holder. It sits safely at the bottom of the ice lantern and lights up the whole lantern.

#2: CONTAIN THE CANDLE

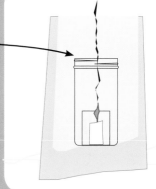

Place the candle in the bottom of a tall, fire-resistant container within the ice lantern. The container's smaller opening helps deflect the wind. If the container is glass, keep in mind that the candle will heat up the glass. When the candle goes out, the container will freeze into the ice and could break if removed. To prevent that, put a plastic lid under the container.

#3: MAKE A NEW CHIMNEY

Flip the ice lantern so that the large opening faces down and drill a new chimney through the top. Position a candle underneath. This method is so effective in blocking the wind that air flow must be increased to sustain the candle. Create a channel in the snow under the lantern or place the lantern over a small stick. You can also drill a small hole into the side near the bottom.

CHIMNEY OPTION A: DRILL WITH FLAME

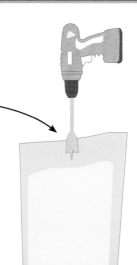

Place an ice lantern open side down over a lit candle (on a nonflammable surface) and the candle will drill its own chimney. This can be done by putting a lit candle in a candle holder on a wire cooling rack in a sink or bathtub and covering it with the ice lantern, large opening down. The wire rack will allow for air flow and the bathtub will catch the melting ice. Once a hole has been created, the lantern is ready for display.

This is my preferred method.

CHIMNEY OPTION B: DRILL WITH POWER DRILL

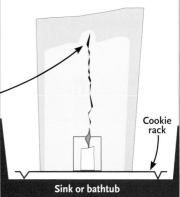

A drill with a 1" spade bit creates a quick chimney. Use care when drilling in ice — it can be slippery. Drill slowly until the drill bit catches in the ice and keep hands clear of the bit. Once a hole has been created, the lantern is ready for display.

CANDLES, continued

Setting Up on Different Surfaces

When using the drilled chimney method *(see p 54)*, the surface on which your ice lanterns will be placed should determine how you prep them for lighting with candles. Here are a few examples showing ice lantern set-ups on varying surfaces.

Moldable

A moldable surface (dry snow, wet snow or dry floral foam) offers many advantages:
It helps level an ice lantern.
It enables creation of a channel to provide air to the candle.
It can also seal the bottom of an ice lantern to keep wind out.

Hard

There are two ways to handle hard surfaces (ice, cement, frozen ground, wood or glass). You can create a hole in the lantern's bottom edge. Or you can prop up one edge with a small stick. Both methods allow air to enter and melting ice to escape.

Supported

A surface made of small rough-edged pieces can be ideal for delivering air to a lantern candle. Examples: wood chips, small rough gravel or a wreath.

Safety Note: Melting ice on concrete sidewalks can create a safely hazard if water refreezes.

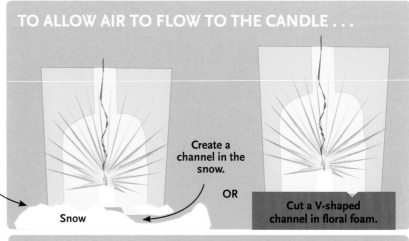

TO ALLOW AIR TO FLOW TO THE CANDLE . . .

Create a channel in the snow.

Snow

OR

Cut a V-shaped channel in floral foam.

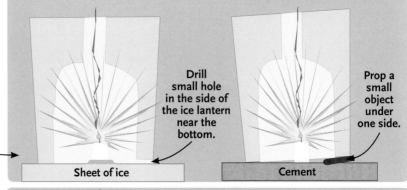

Drill small hole in the side of the ice lantern near the bottom.

Sheet of ice

Prop a small object under one side.

Cement

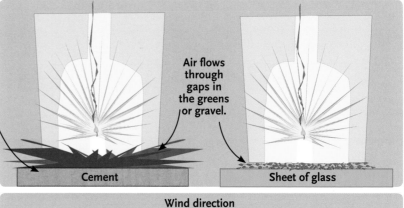

Air flows through gaps in the greens or gravel.

Cement

Sheet of glass

Wind direction

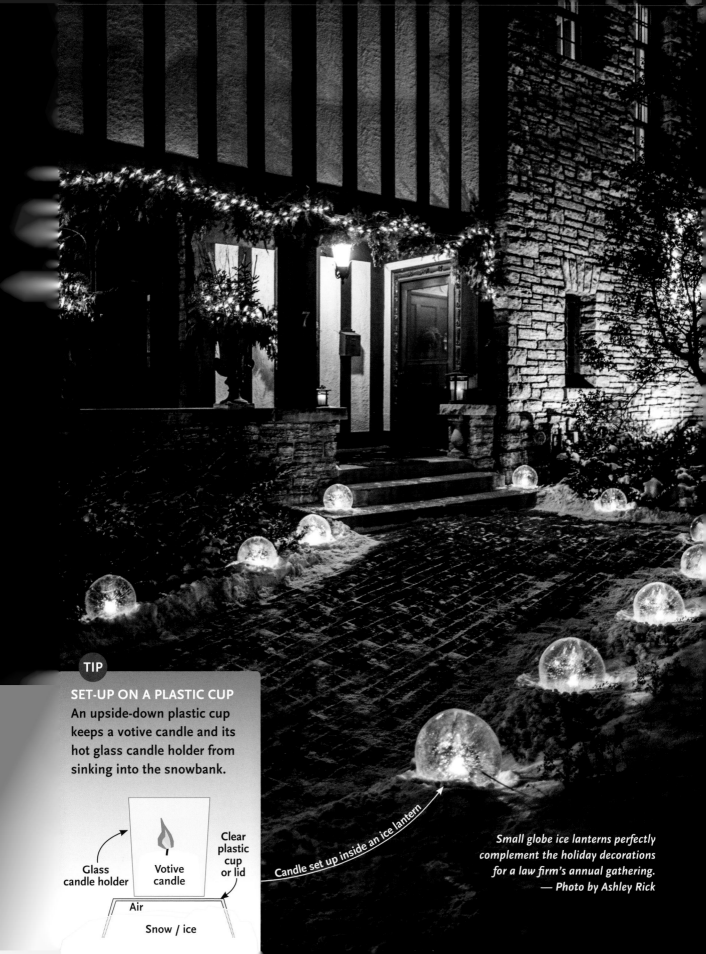

TIP

SET-UP ON A PLASTIC CUP
An upside-down plastic cup keeps a votive candle and its hot glass candle holder from sinking into the snowbank.

Glass candle holder

Votive candle

Clear plastic cup or lid

Air

Snow / ice

Candle set up inside an ice lantern

Small globe ice lanterns perfectly complement the holiday decorations for a law firm's annual gathering.
— Photo by Ashley Rick

EASY BEAUTY with LED LIGHTS *Using LED lights is the easiest way to light up an ice lantern and add color. Just stuff outdoor and/or waterproof LED lights in the lantern opening and walk away. You can even add a timer so they go on every day at dusk.*

Battery-Operated
- Best for indoor applications
- Bright and colorful
- Best for short-term use
- Many color and white options
- Remote control alternatives
- Waterproof choices

LED lights work well for colorful events needing convenient set up — indoors and outdoors. They also work well for indoor applications where open flames aren't allowed.

Crystal lights with wire strings are my favorite.

These globe ice lanterns are lit using long strings of LED icicle lights. The white cords are easily hidden under the snow.

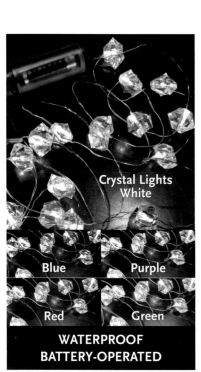

Crystal Lights White

Blue   Purple

Red   Green

WATERPROOF BATTERY-OPERATED

Projection Lights
- Rotating color
- Use indoors and outdoors
- Many colors and white
- Bright, colorful moving light

Use a combo of purple, green and red lights to create a beautiful Northern Lights effect.

PROJECTION LIGHTS

Plug-in String Lights
- Improved technology
- White cords disappear
- Waterproof

Stuff strings of colorful LED lights inside the cavity of an ice lantern to create the easiest and most economical colorful ice show. Lights labeled "outdoor" and "cool touch" work best within cold, wet ice lanterns.

STRINGS OF COLOR

Kids discover "dragon eggs" (globe ice lanterns lit with LED lights) in the walls of an ice castle at the Mall of America. This creative company, Ice Castles, LLC, employs master builders who have perfected the art of spraying water over icicles to grow glacial cathedrals around the world. — *Photo by Rob Enedy*

SIMPLE MAGIC with SUNLIGHT *Ice put in the sun melts, yes.*
But the sunlight finds small imperfections and deepens them. Once the ice refreezes overnight,
daylight will pour through the newly cut crystal and dance for joy.

Sunlight works like candle-light or LED light, passing right through clear ice. But when it hits a crack in the ice or a dense field of frozen minerals and gases, it bounces around and glows.

In creating luminaries, I try to hit the middle ground. I like ice that is clear with lines of minerals through it. This ensures the light will both bounce around *and* shine through the lanterns.

Simply place your ice creation on cement or, if it needs help to stand tall, perch it in a pile of snow. As long as it's sitting in the sun, it will be amazing.

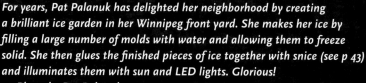

For years, Pat Palanuk has delighted her neighborhood by creating a brilliant ice garden in her Winnipeg front yard. She makes her ice by filling a large number of molds with water and allowing them to freeze solid. She then glues the finished pieces of ice together with snice (see p 43) and illuminates them with sun and LED lights. Glorious!
— Photo by Pat Palanuk

This drip tray system has a large flat-bottomed brass bowl with a green glass riser. Rough deco-glass stabilizes the ice lantern and provides air flow for the candle inside. Faux branches fill the bowl and leave lots of room for melting ice. This centerpiece will last 5-10 hours indoors.
— Photo by Jennifer Shea Hedberg

DRIP TRAY COMBINATIONS

The globe ice lantern centerpiece at left is one of many indoor display possibilities. You can change the bowl, riser, decorations, and use a different ice lantern shape. All these alternatives will bring unique charm to your table.

BOWLS

A bowl for an ice lantern centerpiece must be able to hold all the melting ice. Before using it at an event, create an ice lantern and let it begin melting into the bowl of your choice to make sure it will not overflow. I have used a punch bowl, a large dog dish, a vintage bait bucket, a chicken feed pan, a large planter filled with dirt and many other receptacles. The common denominator is that they all hold enough water.

RISERS

The purpose of a riser is to hold the ice lantern above the melting ice. This will help slow the melting process and keep the candle from drowning. Over the years I have used many things — tiered cake plates, a short wood log, a paint can with holes punched in the top, and a rock-filled container — but I love floral foam risers. The trick is to use floral foam that is meant to be soaked, but do keep it dry so that it will absorb the melting ice. Keep in mind that some fresh flowers will need to be put into water-filled floral tubes (see p 66) and then inserted into the dry foam to look their best and last the duration of your event.

DECORATIONS

Think wisely about how much space your decorations will take up in the bowl. The stems of flowers can displace more water than you might imagine. Try using a wreath that rests on the edge of the bowl, leaving more room for melting ice.

ICE LANTERNS OF ANY SHAPE

A globe-shaped ice lantern sitting in a wreath nest is beautiful, but any shape ice lantern in a well-chosen bowl will be lovely.

Globe ice lantern on a glass tiered cake plate with fresh flowers in a cut crystal bowl

Floral foam riser with a hard foam top

Globe ice lantern on a foam riser in a pumpkin bowl

Balloon in bucket ice lantern on a foam riser arranged in a 9" x 12" baking pan with fresh flowers

✳ Indoor Ice Luminary Display

This project offers just one of many possible combinations for creating a drip-tray system that can be used to stage an ice lantern on a food table or entryway. The bowl is a galvanized stock pan from a farm supply store. The floral foam riser provides a stable platform for the candlelit globe ice lantern and helps secure the faux flowers. Try your hand at this starter project, then let your imagination run free.

1 GLOBE ICE LANTERN

Drilled chimney

2 BOWL

STEP 1: Make a small globe ice lantern *(see p 29)*. Place it with the large opening down, and, if you plan to use a candle, create a chimney with a power drill and spade bit (1"-1.5"). Set aside on a piece of plastic in be-low-freezing temps until ready to use. (More chimney drilling information can be found on page 54.)

STEP 2: Choose a bowl that can hold the amount of water you'll use to make your ice lantern. To check the bowl's capacity, fill your chosen balloon or bucket to the desired size and then pour the water into the bowl. If the bowl can hold all that water, then it will hold most of the melting ice plus any flowers or other decorations.

Left: The bowl for this centerpiece is a galvanized aluminum stock pan. It's relatively inexpensive, has a stable bottom, and can present a rustic look or be easily dressed up with ribbon and flowers.
— *Photo by Jennifer Shea Hedberg*

3 RISER IN BOWL

4 DECORATE BOWL

5 DECORATE RISER

STEP 3: Add a dry floral foam riser to the bowl. *Do not presoak the foam.*

STEP 4: If the bowl you've chosen needs to be dressed up, a bit of ribbon is a nice touch. Follow your own instincts.

STEP 5: Choose some flowers (real or faux) and push the ends into the foam to create an arrangement. If you want to use real flowers, see below.

USING REAL FLOWERS?

Real flowers need a supply of water to keep them happy and healthy before and during your event. Two choices:

PRESOAK THE FOAM RISER. Insert your fresh flowers into the moist foam. WARNING! The downside of this technique is that your bowl will need to be considerably larger to accommodate the water you've added to soak the floral foam.

USE FLORAL TUBES WITH UNSOAKED FLORAL FOAM. Insert each fresh flower stem into a floral tube filled with water. Push the floral tubes with the flowers into the dry foam. The dry foam will help soak up melting ice.

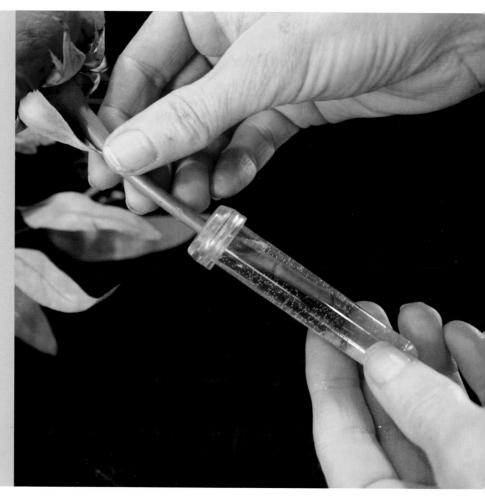

6 ILLUMINATE

Carve groove
when using a
candle

7 ADD GLOBE

STEP 6: If using a candle, make sure to cut a groove into the foam top with an exacto knife. The ice lantern will adhere to the foam and become firmly attached. The groove will supply the candle with needed oxygen — and allow melting ice to flow away from the candle.

If using a waterproof, battery-operated LED light, there's no need to carve a groove into the foam.

STEP 7: About 30 minutes before the event starts, light the candle and put the globe ice lantern over the candle with the large opening down and the flame directly under the drilled chimney. (LED lights? Put the globe over the lights.) Make sure the centerpiece feels stable, then go greet your guests.

TIP

OVERFLOW WARNING
Remember to check your centerpiece from time to time to make sure the water level in the bowl is ok.

I like to keep a turkey baster and a small bucket handy to avert disaster. If too much water accumulates, insert the baster into the bowl and suction out enough water to keep the centerpiece from overflowing.

Also consider using an "insurance policy" — a large low-profile container underneath your indoor display to catch any unexpected water overflow.

CREATING OUTDOOR DISPLAYS *For outdoor ice luminary artistry that captivates, think outside the lined walkway and consider these design alternative ideas.*

Lined Walkways

If you're planning to line a walkway with ice luminaries, consider putting them just off the path. Then the melting ice will flow into the snow or ground and not onto the cement where it could refreeze and create a walking hazard.

Design Asymmetrically

Many people assume balanced means symmetrical. But a great way to make a display feel peaceful is to use asymmetrical balance. Try lining a walkway only on one side, alternating ice lanterns to cover the same distance with less, or putting one large stunning ice lantern on one side and balancing it with several smaller lanterns.

Dark Spots

It's easy for the light of an ice lantern to get washed out by the light of a front porch or other outdoor lights. If possible, go outside the night before and mark the darker spots. Those are the areas where ice lanterns will really shine.

Focal Point

If you have a limited supply of ice lanterns, one of which is spectacular, start by spacing out the ice lanterns a few at a time

An ice flower serves as an ideal focal point for this ice luminary display.
— Photo by Jennifer Shea Hedberg

and far apart, then place them closer together, then closer still — until you dazzle visitors with your biggest or most beautiful ice luminary.

Multi-Level Ice

A surefire way to impress is to go vertical with your ice. Create tall ice lanterns, stack small ice lanterns, or use tall ice glass to direct the light upward. Building with ice is delightfully challenging — especially when lighting with candles.

Finishing Touches

Snow stops light. After the last lantern is placed, consider using a paint scraper to remove extra snow. Then with a torch use sweeping motions back and forth from the top down to remove any snowy haze that will dim the light. It will make the ice sparkle. (More finishing instructions on p 72.)

After lining the walkway of this house (see left) with 16 ice lanterns, I noticed a snow-covered patio table under a white canopy. It was a perfect spot for an eye-catching luminary, so I made an ice flower (see p 169) with a few left-over pieces of ice glass. — Photo by Jennifer Shea Hedberg

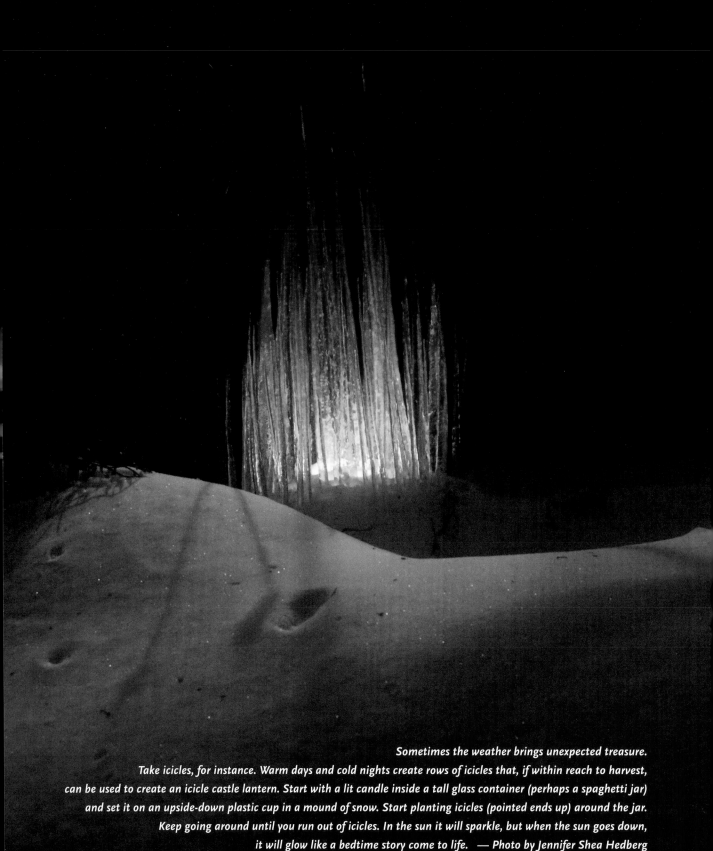

Sometimes the weather brings unexpected treasure.
Take icicles, for instance. Warm days and cold nights create rows of icicles that, if within reach to harvest,
can be used to create an icicle castle lantern. Start with a lit candle inside a tall glass container (perhaps a spaghetti jar)
and set it on an upside-down plastic cup in a mound of snow. Start planting icicles (pointed ends up) around the jar.
Keep going around until you run out of icicles. In the sun it will sparkle, but when the sun goes down,
it will glow like a bedtime story come to life. — *Photo by Jennifer Shea Hedberg*

WORKING with WEATHER *It used to be we could rely on good cold weather up here in Minnesota, but lately that's not true. I've started offering my clients the guarantee that I will do the most I can considering the weather conditions of the day.*

What's the Forecast?

Look at the weather ahead when hatching your ice luminary plans. Here are four scenarios.

A Snow on the ground and temps near 8°F is the best scenario. It's possible to make, store and display anything, especially ice glass. You'll have snow to insulate and temps cold enough to make even large ice creations.

B No snow on the ground and temps around 8°F. Frozen ground will still insulate, so ice lanterns can be frozen and lit.

C Snow on the ground and temps above 15°F is tricky, but it's still possible to create something fun. Watch for a short cold snap of temps less than 10°F. Then make small ice lanterns, wrap them in plastic bags and store in freezers or under piles of snow (in the shade) until ready to use. The ice lanterns should last for one evening of delight.

The photo at right shows an example of a "C" scenario. I made thick, beautiful tiny globes and thin, clear extra-large globe ice lanterns. I put one inside the other for a fantastic focal point.

Warm temps can yield beautiful tiny globe ice lanterns and thin, clear extra-large globe ice lanterns. In a pinch, combine the two for this incandescent effect.
— *Photo by Jennifer Shea Hedberg*

D No snow on the ground and temps above 32°F require freezer space. If you have a large display planned, you may need to find sympathetic friends with freezer space. You'll need to make and store ice lanterns in a freezer. Expect your display to last only for one night.

Set up in Rain/Snow

Use LED lights. If you need to use candles, use the drilled chimney method *(see p 54)* and never leave an unlit candle exposed to moisture.

FINISHING TOUCHES *The appearance and integrity of ice glass and ice luminaries can be enhanced with a few simple techniques. Taking the time to fine-tune your creations can make your final display all the more spectacular.*

Using Heat

The best way to effect subtle change with ice is to apply heat. Effective tools include flowing hot/cold tap water, a clothes iron, a sink bottom, a hair dryer and a torch. In a pinch, I've used a hot glue gun, a wood-burning tool and a curling iron. Heat is useful for all sorts of finishing tasks:

Making repairs

An ice lantern can sometimes freeze strangely. Its opening or cavity might too small, or it may be misshapen in some way. If the lantern will sit on a hard surface such as ice or cement, its bottom may need to be flattened so it sits straight.

Prepping ice for assembly

The best way to glue two pieces of ice together is with two wet, flat surfaces and cold temps.

Making it sparkle

After ice has formed, it might develop a light-blurring haze on its surface caused by moving from cold to hot air temps. When you take the ice outside again, the haze will remain unless you remove it with heat.

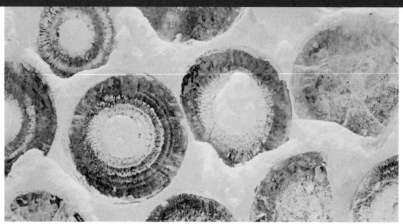

Frozen-solid cylinders of ice are sliced with a chain saw and then assembled into a stained glass ice wall with snice. — Photo by Jennifer Shea Hedberg

Cutting and Slicing

When a dramatic change is needed, such as slicing ice or carving a door in an ice castle wall, I use larger electric tools such as a chain saw or Sawzall and finish with a torch or hair dryer. For example, I cut bucket ice lanterns that have frozen solid into thick slices (*see above*) and arrange them with snice into an ice wall. When light shines through, it looks like stained glass.

Which Tool?

Flowing hot/cold tap water

- Reshapes and removes ice quickly, but is hard to control.
- Makes large holes — fast.

Flat-bottomed sink

- Removes and flattens ice.

Clothes iron

- Makes rough surfaces flat.
- Levels larger surfaces (with aluminum sheet and level).
- Makes indentations in ice using the edge of the iron.

Hair dryers and torches

- Dry heat removes haze from ice lanterns and restores the shine and clarity of pure ice.
- A torch is handy for outdoors. I use a Bernzomatic MAP-Pro Hose Torch Kit.

Other heat producing tools

If you own something that can safely be used to apply heat to ice, give it a try.

At the end of assembly day for the Middlemoon Creekwalk, volunteers focus on lighting candles. It can take several hours to light the hundreds of luminaries at the festival.
— Photo by Larry Risser

PART 4: Ice Projects

— Photo by Jennifer Shea Hedberg

Changing the Shape

If a water-tight container is filled with water and allowed to partially freeze, the resulting ice lantern will take on the shape and contours of that container. There are many ways to create new and interesting lantern shapes by going beyond the bucket.

CONSIDER THE POSSIBILITIES:

Shaped Containers

It's easiest to pick a waterproof container with an interesting shape to fill with water and partially freeze. (Make sure the top is bigger than the bottom so the ice can slide out.) A Bundt pan — normally used to make cakes — is a perfect example. I use two of these pans to make the *Bundt Pan Ice Cake Lantern* (*see p 79*). They can be found in many shapes and sizes and are almost always designed with a central tube that creates a ready-made chimney.

Flexible Containers

If the container you choose can be manipulated, it's possible to create an altered-shape ice lantern by flexing the container and holding it in that position while it freezes. The *Teardrop Ice Lantern* (*see p 83*) is a great example of this concept.

Constrained Flexibility

If a balloon is filled with water while it's inside a hard-sided container, the ice lantern formed will resemble the shape of that container, but with added height and softer edges. This concept is demonstrated in the *Balloon in Bucket Ice Lantern* (*see p 87*).

Constrained Dimensions

The previous project alters the overall shape of an ice lantern. The *Celery Stalk Ice Lantern* (*see p 91*) shows how the dimensions of the ice can be further altered by placing 3-dimensional items in between the balloon and the bucket.

Super Flex!

The *Super Stretchy Ice Lantern* (*see p 95*) takes the idea of altering shape to a new level using jumbo puffer balls. These balloon toys are incredibly flexible and surprisingly strong, so they squeeze into crevices regular balloons can't.

This beautiful ice lantern nested in a floral centerpiece was created by filling a balloon with water inside a dollar-store plastic vase using the partial-freeze method (see p 19). — Photo by Jennifer Shea Hedberg

BUNDT PAN ICE CAKE LANTERN

TEARDROP ICE LANTERN

BALLOON IN BUCKET ICE LANTERN

CELERY STALK ICE LANTERN

SUPER STRETCHY ICE LANTERN

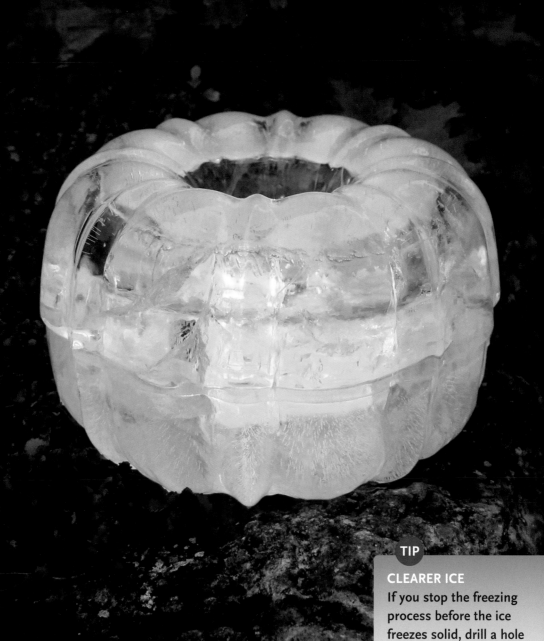

TIP

CLEARER ICE
If you stop the freezing process before the ice freezes solid, drill a hole in the top and release the water. Use as is, or replace with fresh water and let it freeze solid.

✳ Bundt Pan Ice Cake Lantern

WHAT YOU NEED

2 Bundt pans

Cold tap water

Cold temps
or deep freezer

Candle
in candle holder

Matches

Nearly everyone has Bundt pans or can find them, so the ice lanterns they make are perfect for a flash mob ice lantern festival. I gave this idea a test at the Middlemoon Creekwalk, a pop-up event my husband Tom and I created a few years ago. One year I asked that any willing neighbor with a Bundt pan fill it with water, let it freeze solid and bring the ice to me. I assembled the gathered ice into a lavish collection of luminaries for the event. It was thrilling to see so many people answer the call to populate the creekside with glowing ice cakes!

Bundt pans can be found in many different sizes and shapes — from ginger-bread houses and miniature pine forests to flower shapes and castles. Large Bundt pans can be used alone as ice lantern molds. Two or more together make a charming form of convoluted ice that protects a candle's flame and sparks the imagination.

To help illustrate, I made the Bundt pans see-through.

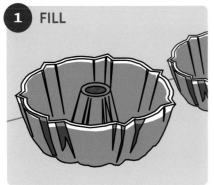

1 FILL

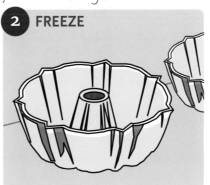

2 FREEZE

STEP 1: Fill 2 Bundt pans with tap water to within .5" from the top and place them in a freezer or outdoors on cement, stone, metal — any surface that conducts cold. **Why?** The bottom of the pan is where the decorative shaping is located.

STEP 2: Allow the water to freeze solid. (**Warning!** When water freezes solid it expands, so the ice will likely crack. If your Bundt pans are made of thin plastic, they could crack as well.)

12 HOURS at 0°F

— *Photos by Jennifer Shea Hedberg*

3 RELEASE

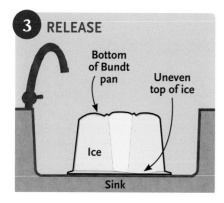

Bottom of Bundt pan

Uneven top of ice

Ice

Sink

STEP 3: Place one Bundt pan upside down in a sink and wait a few minutes for the ice to thaw enough for the pan to be lifted off. Wrap the piece of ice in a plastic bag and place it in below-freezing temps. Repeat with the second Bundt pan.

4 LEVEL TOP

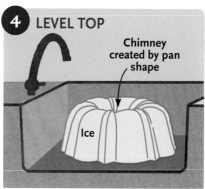

Chimney created by pan shape

Ice

Sink

STEP 4: When water freezes it expands, so the top of the ice is usually uneven — surging to one side. To fuse the two Bundt pan-shaped ice pieces, it's helpful to first flatten the top surfaces. (When the surfaces are flat, there is less chance for wind to enter and blow out the candle.)

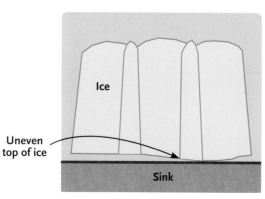

Ice

Uneven top of ice

Sink

To flatten ice: Heat up the bottom of a sink by filling it with hot water and then releasing the water down the drain. Hold ice as level as possible on the sink bottom so the high point of the ice touches the sink first. As the point of ice melts, the top will become flatter.

Repeat with the second Bundt pan-shaped ice piece.

5 ASSEMBLE / GLUE

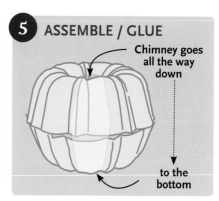

Chimney goes all the way down

to the bottom

STEP 5: Wet the two flat ice surfaces and position them together. Put the combined ice in below-freezing temps for at least an hour (if above 8°F) to "glue" or freeze together.

6 LIGHT

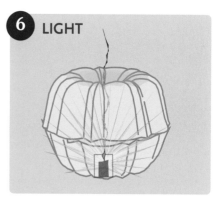

STEP 6: Place a candle in a candle holder (or LED light) on the ground and lower the lantern over the candle. Check for air flow and enjoy the glow!

TIP

CANDLE CLEARANCE
If the Bundt pan ice cake lantern's chimney is not large enough for a votive candle in a candle holder, run hot water through the hole to expand it.

Stacked Bundt pan ice cake lanterns made with a variety of cake and Jello molds. All ice pieces must be flattened so they'll fit together tightly. This will protect candles from the wind.
— Photo by Jennifer Shea Hedberg

During warmer months, an ice lantern pulled from the freezer can be magical. If it's thick enough and placed in the shade or after sunset, it should last for several hours — or perhaps even all night!

Teardrop Ice Lantern

This stretched globe ice lantern adds whimsy to any ice luminary installation. Releasing air that has entered the balloon while filling it with water is critical for creating a pointed top. Read on page 169 how this lantern makes a perfect ice flower center, too!

To help illustrate, I made the buckets see-through.

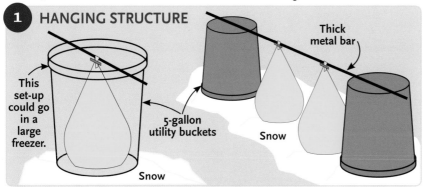

1 HANGING STRUCTURE

This set-up could go in a large freezer.

5-gallon utility buckets

Thick metal bar

Snow

Snow

STEP 1: Create a hanging structure strong enough to hold the weight of a standard punching balloon filled with water. Keep in mind that the balloon, while hanging, must touch the snow or ground to insulate its bottom from the cold. A trip to a hardware store will reveal other options for building a hanging system: a long steel bolt (1/2"), a piece of rebar, or a metal shelf support.

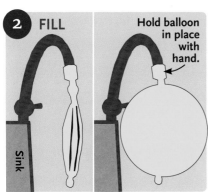

2 FILL

Hold balloon in place with hand.

Sink

Be sure to hold the punching balloon tightly around the faucet head while filling with water.

STEP 2: Fill a standard punching balloon with warm tap water by stretching its mouth around the water faucet head to form a seal. Hold it tightly in place with thumb and forefinger as it fills to the desired size. Release any air that has risen to the top of the balloon and clip closed until ready to hang.

Warning! Hot water will make the punching balloon more elastic (good for this application), but it can also weaken the latex and be hot to the touch.

3 TIE | CLIP

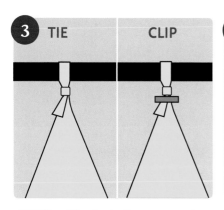

4 FREEZE

12
11   1
10   **24**   2
9 HOURS 3
8 at **0**°F 4
7   5
6

5 PEEL AND RELEASE

STEP 3: Tie the balloon around your hanging bar or rod and close the clip under the knot. Make sure the bottom of the balloon touches the ground or snow.

STEP 4: Let the water-filled balloon freeze for around 24 hours or until a strong crust of ice has formed inside the balloon.

STEP 5: With a pair of scissors or sharp knife, cut the balloon free of the support bar. Slice the balloon and peel it off the ice. The water that did not freeze will come gushing out the open bottom.

6 ADD LIGHT

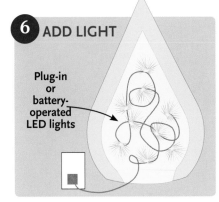

Plug-in or battery-operated LED lights

STEP 6: Teardrop ice lanterns require special lighting strategies. Their signature look is the pointed top, so it makes sense to display them in a way that takes advantage of that aspect. Use LED lights for a fast, easy, and colorful option.

6 ALT: DRILL AN OFFSET CHIMNEY FOR A CANDLE

Candles need a chimney.

Start drilling at this angle.

ALT STEP 6: The heat from a candle goes straight up, so use a power dill and spade bit to create an offset chimney that preserves the pointed top.
Note: Using a candle to create a chimney will **NOT** work with a teardrop ice lantern.

Preserve the lantern's pointed top by drilling an offset chimney. Begin drilling flat to the ice just until the bit penetrates (*see above*). Then angle the drill up and drill straight down (*see below*).

Finish drilling at this angle.

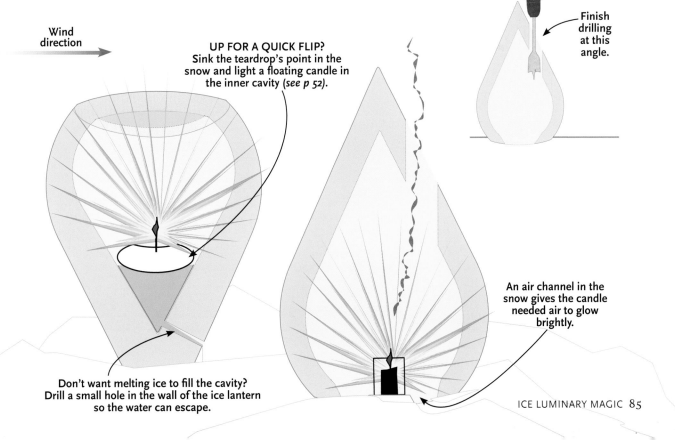

Wind direction

UP FOR A QUICK FLIP?
Sink the teardrop's point in the snow and light a floating candle in the inner cavity (*see p 52*).

Don't want melting ice to fill the cavity? Drill a small hole in the wall of the ice lantern so the water can escape.

An air channel in the snow gives the candle needed air to glow brightly.

— *Photo by Bob Hays*

6 ADD LIGHT

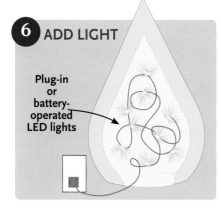

Plug-in or battery-operated LED lights

STEP 6: Teardrop ice lanterns require special lighting strategies. Their signature look is the pointed top, so it makes sense to display them in a way that takes advantage of that aspect. Use LED lights for a fast, easy, and colorful option.

6 ALT: DRILL AN OFFSET CHIMNEY FOR A CANDLE

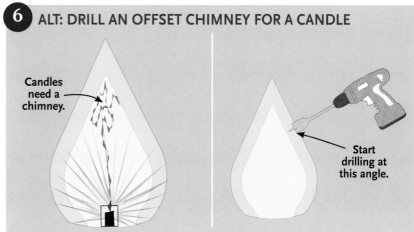

Candles need a chimney.

Start drilling at this angle.

ALT STEP 6: The heat from a candle goes straight up, so use a power dill and spade bit to create an offset chimney that preserves the pointed top. *Note:* Using a candle to create a chimney will **NOT** work with a teardrop ice lantern.

Preserve the lantern's pointed top by drilling an offset chimney. Begin drilling flat to the ice just until the bit penetrates *(see above)*. Then angle the drill up and drill straight down *(see below)*.

Finish drilling at this angle.

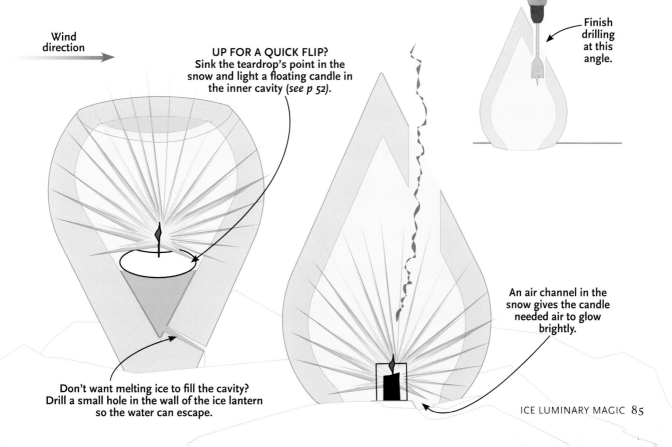

Wind direction

UP FOR A QUICK FLIP?
Sink the teardrop's point in the snow and light a floating candle in the inner cavity *(see p 52)*.

An air channel in the snow gives the candle needed air to glow brightly.

Don't want melting ice to fill the cavity? Drill a small hole in the wall of the ice lantern so the water can escape.

— *Photo by Bob Hays*

Balloon in Bucket Ice Lantern

A standard balloon is meant to be filled with air. When warm water is used instead, the balloon's structure can relax and "blob out." This project takes advantage of that tendency by allowing the rubber to soften within a hard container. Change the size or shape of the hard container or the size of the balloon and the resulting ice lantern changes, too. This shape-changing strategy offers many interesting possibilities.

To help illustrate, I made the bucket see-through.

1 **BALLOON**

2 **FILL**

Hold the balloon in place with your hand as it fills with water.

STEP 1: Stretch the balloon's mouth around a water faucet head or garden hose to form a seal. Hold the balloon tightly in place with thumb and forefinger. Make sure the balloon is inside the container and then slowly turn on the water.

STEP 2: Fill the balloon with warm tap water while keeping the balloon inside the bucket. Turn off the water when the balloon has achieved the look and size desired. Note how the balloon starts to "blob out" over the edges of the small bucket.

TRY

BUCKETS AND BALLOONS

Vary the size of the bucket relative to the balloon to create different effects.

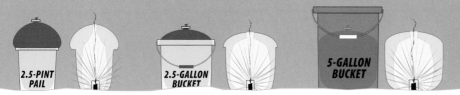

2.5-PINT PAIL

2.5-GALLON BUCKET

5-GALLON BUCKET

Use different balloon sizes for even more experimentation.

3 CLIP AND INSULATE

Snow

STEP 3: Secure the balloon with an easy-close clip or tie it closed.

Place the bucket on insulation, snow or frozen ground so the water in the bucket's bottom remains unfrozen.

4 FREEZE

18 HOURS at 0°F

STEP 4: Freeze for around 18 hours or until a strong crust of ice forms inside the balloon. If you use a larger bucket or temps are warmer than 0°F, the freezing time will be longer. Conversely, if you use a smaller bucket or temps are colder than 0°F, the freezing time will be shorter.

5 THAW

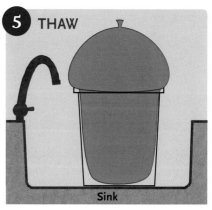

Sink

STEP 5: Remove the clip and let the bucket sit in the sink for 15-30 minutes. Tip the bucket and balloon upside down until the balloon-covered ice slides out.

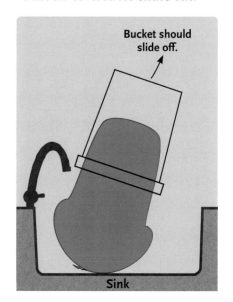

Bucket should slide off.

Sink

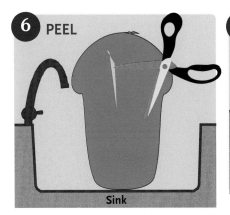

6 PEEL

Sink

STEP 6: With a pair of scissors or sharp knife, slice the balloon and peel it off the ice.

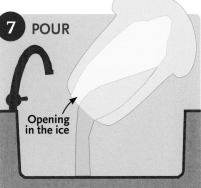

7 POUR

Opening in the ice

STEP 7: The water that did not freeze will come gushing out the open bottom. (If the bottom is frozen, it can easily be chipped open using a knife or screwdriver.) Pour out any remaining water.

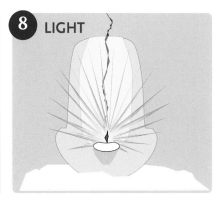

8 LIGHT

STEP 8: When you're ready to use the ice lantern, place a candle inside it and light. I love to use floating candles if the lantern doesn't have an outlet to release the melting ice.

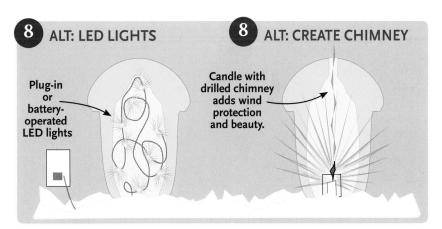

8 ALT: LED LIGHTS

Plug-in or battery-operated LED lights

8 ALT: CREATE CHIMNEY

Candle with drilled chimney adds wind protection and beauty.

ALT STEP 8: Fill the cavity of the ice lantern with LED lights intended for outdoor use. Place it on the ground in the desired location and turn on the lights.

ALT STEP 8: The magic of a candle, the beauty of the ice and better wind protection makes this alternative ideal. Another step is required to create a chimney, but it's well worth it. (Chimney instructions, p 54.)

Celery Stalk Ice Lantern

When a balloon is filled with water inside a bucket and 3-D objects are placed between the balloon and the bucket, those objects will alter the shape of the balloon and thus the shape of the eventual ice lantern. In this project, I'll fill a stretchy balloon with warm tap water to increase its flexibility and then use celery stalks to influence its shape. Why celery? It's inexpensive, organically shaped and can be added to soup after the lantern is made!

To help illustrate, I made the large bucket see-through.

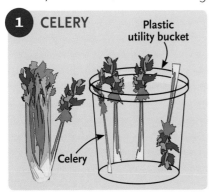

1 CELERY

Plastic utility bucket

Celery

2 FILL

Garden hose

STEP 1: Peel the stalks from the celery bunch. Line the inside of the bucket with the celery stalks. Don't worry if the stalks fall over. You can adjust them as the balloon fills the bucket. To make the shape of the finished ice lantern more interesting, try to space the celery stalks irregularly and leave spots where the balloon can touch the bucket.

STEP 2: Stretch the mouth of a standard punching balloon around the head of a faucet or garden hose to form a seal. Place the bucket so the balloon is inside it. While holding the balloon tightly with thumb and forefinger, begin to fill it with warm tap water. Once the balloon starts to push the celery stalks against the inside of the bucket, turn off the water to adjust the celery stalks as needed. Turn on the water and continue filling the balloon to the desired shape and size.

Left: This beautiful photo of a celery stalk ice lantern lit by the sun was taken during the set-up day for the Middlemoon Creekwalk by Bob Hays, a friend, neighbor and photographer.

WHAT YOU NEED

Standard punching balloon

2-gallon plastic utility bucket

One bunch of celery

Warm tap water

Easy-close clip

Cold temps or deep freezer

Candle in candle holder

Matches

3 FILL

STEP 3: Tie or clip the balloon closed.

4 FREEZE

24 HOURS at 0°F

STEP 4: Freeze for about 24 hours or until a strong crust of ice has formed inside the balloon.

5 THAW

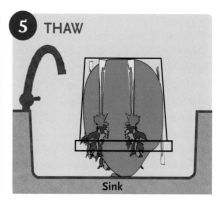

Sink

STEP 5: Remove the clip and let the balloon sit in the sink for 15-30 minutes. Tip the bucket upside down until the balloon and the celery slide out.

Balloon and celery in a utility bucket, set to freeze on the snow.

Celery stalk ice lantern displayed with large opening down, a chimney drilled through the top and lit with a candle.

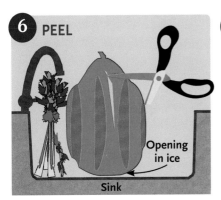

6 PEEL

Opening in ice

Sink

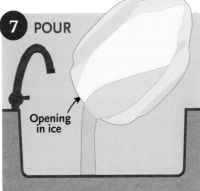

7 POUR

Opening in ice

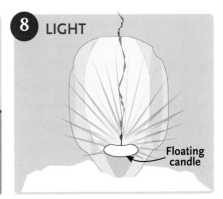

8 LIGHT

Floating candle

STEP 6: Peel off the frozen celery. With a pair of scissors or sharp knife, make a slice in the balloon and peel it off the ice.

STEP 7: The water that did not freeze may come gushing out the open bottom. (If not, the bottom can easily be chipped open using a knife or screwdriver.) Pour the extra water from the ice lantern.

STEP 8: When you're ready to display the ice lantern, place a floating candle in the bottom of the lantern. Light it up!

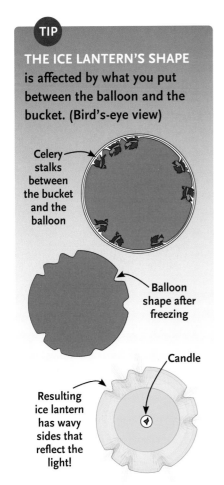

TIP

THE ICE LANTERN'S SHAPE is affected by what you put between the balloon and the bucket. (Bird's-eye view)

Celery stalks between the bucket and the balloon

Balloon shape after freezing

Candle

Resulting ice lantern has wavy sides that reflect the light!

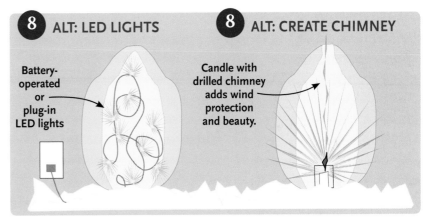

8 ALT: LED LIGHTS

Battery-operated or plug-in LED lights

8 ALT: CREATE CHIMNEY

Candle with drilled chimney adds wind protection and beauty.

ALT STEP 8: Fill the cavity of the ice lantern with a string of LED lights intended for outdoor use. Place it on the ground with the large opening facing down and turn on the lights.

ALT STEP 8: The magic of a candle, the beauty of the ice and better wind protection make this a great alternative. Another step is required to create a chimney, but it's well worth it *(see p 54)*.

*Super stretchy ice lantern
displayed with the large
opening down
and a drilled chimney.
— Photo by Jennifer Shea Hedberg*

Super Stretchy Ice Lantern

When filled with water, a jumbo puffer ball becomes a giant blob, so it must be supported by a hard structure. Perforated aluminum sheets will provide that support, but not before they are bent into flowing waves and put into a utility bucket for even more support.

WHAT YOU NEED

2 • 12" x 24" perforated aluminum sheets

3-4 paper fasteners or small zip ties

5-gallon plastic utility bucket

Broom handle or 1" x 24" PVC pipe

Jumbo puffer ball or other super stretchy rubber ball

Warm tap water

Large easy-close clip

Cold temps or deep freezer

Candle in candle holder

Matches

1 METAL

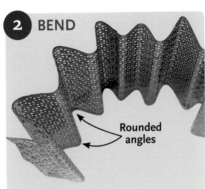

Paper Fasteners

STEP 1: Put the short ends of 2 aluminum sheets together and overlap about 1". Poke paper fasteners (or small plastic zip ties) through the holes in the metal and open the prongs to hold the aluminum sheets together.

2 BEND

Rounded angles

STEP 2: Use a broom handle or thin PVC pipe to help make round bends in the aluminum sheets.

TIP

PAPER FASTENERS 101
Shaped somewhat like a nail, a paper fastener has a round head and two flexible prongs that can pierce sheets of paper or metal and then bend to hold them together.

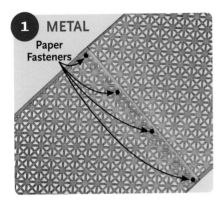

24" 24"

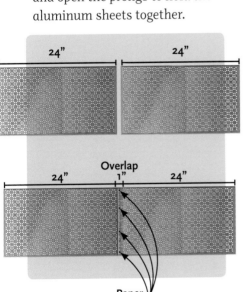

Overlap 1"
24" 24"

Paper Fasteners

3 PLACE IN BUCKET

4 POKE HOLE IN BALL

Make a VERY
small hole!

5 FILL PUFFER BALL AND CLIP CLOSED

STEP 3: Fit the bent metal into the bucket. Wrap one end of the metal into the other end and adjust as necessary. Make sure any balloon-popping metal points are facing out toward the bucket.

STEP 4: A puffer ball doesn't come with a hole, so a small hole must be cut into the ball.

Lower the puffer ball into the metal form before filling

Stretch the hole of the puffer ball around the head of a faucet or garden hose and hold tightly with thumb and forefinger. Place the bucket so the puffer ball is inside it.

STEP 5: Fill the puffer ball with warm tap water while continuing to hold it firmly to the faucet head or hose. Turn off the water when the puffer ball has filled the space. Gather up the rubber around the hole and clip closed.

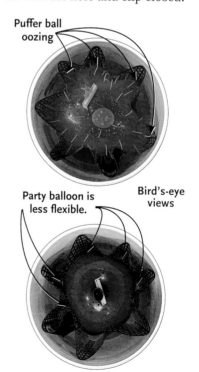

Puffer ball oozing

Party balloon is less flexible.

Bird's-eye views

MORE OOZE? After you fill the puffer ball with water, you'll notice how much more elastic it is than a balloon. To send the puffer ball even further into the contours of the metal form, unclip and fill with a little more water and reclip. Push it down using the lid of the bucket. Keep the lid on while freezing.

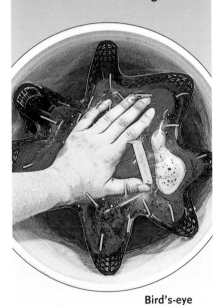

Bird's-eye view

The puffer ball doesn't fill the bucket? Place a piece of Styrofoam or a folded towel on top so the lid requires a little effort to snap into place.

6 FREEZE

24 HOURS at 0°F

STEP 6: Freeze the bucket on an insulated surface for about 24 hours at 0°F or until a strong crust of ice forms inside the puffer ball. If the crust isn't as thick as you'd like, continue to freeze and check every 6 hours. Once the crust feels sufficiently thick, remove the clip on the puffer ball so the hole can be widened for a better view of the ice inside.

7 THAW

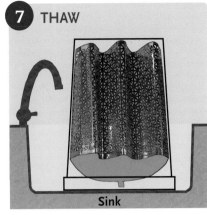

Sink

STEP 7: Let the container sit in the sink for 15-30 minutes. Tip the bucket upside down until the balloon and metal form slide out.

8 UNWRAP METAL

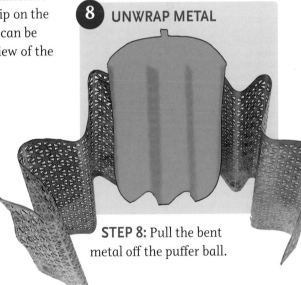

STEP 8: Pull the bent metal off the puffer ball.

9 UNWRAP ICE

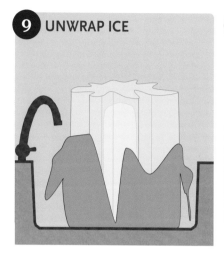

STEP 9: Peel the puffer ball off the ice. The water that did not freeze should gush out of the open bottom.

10 POUR

STEP 10: Pour out any water that remains inside the ice lantern.

11 LIGHT

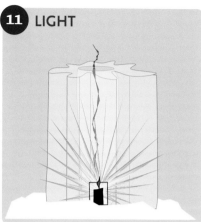

STEP 11: When you're ready to display the lantern, flip it over so the opening in the bottom faces up. Place a floating candle inside the lantern. Light and enjoy the glow!

11 ALT: LED LIGHTS

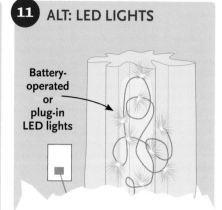

Battery-operated or plug-in LED lights

ALT STEP 11: Fill the lantern's cavity with a string of LED lights intended for outdoor use. Place it on the ground (with the opening facing down) in the desired location and turn on the lights.

11 ALT: CREATE CHIMNEY

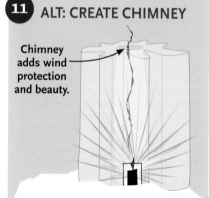

Chimney adds wind protection and beauty.

ALT STEP 11: The magic of a candle, the beauty of the ice and better wind protection make this alternative the best. Another step is required to create a chimney, but it's well worth the effort (*see p 54*).

Adding Texture

One of the magical qualities of ice is its ability to hold and reflect light. When an edge is created in the ice, the light finds it and bounces. The best way to make the light dance is to create as many edges as possible.

CONSIDER THE OPTIONS:

Flat Surfaces

The *Ice Appliqué Lantern* (*see p 103*) project creates edges by gluing one or more pieces of ice onto a lantern. Flattening the ice is the first step, because one flat wet ice surface held against another in cold temps is the best formula for joining ice together. This process fuses the ice on a molecular level.

Cold Temps

The temperature at which two pieces of wet ice will stick together instantly is 8°F. The process for making an *Ice Snowball Lantern* (*see p 109*) is simplified if it can be built at that temperature or colder.

Thicker is Better

When lining a bucket with non-porous material to create a pattern in the ice, it's best if it's relatively thick. Thicker material leaves a deeper impression in the ice. That's why I love using heavy-duty rubber doormats to make the *Doormat Ice Lantern* (*see p 113*). Doormats come in many patterns, are easy to remove from the ice and are stiff enough to stand upright during the freezing process.

Hot Glue

Gluing non-porous items into a bucket to create ice texture is tricky because too much glue makes it hard for the ice to slide out. With the *Plastic Tube Ice Lantern* (*see p 117*) project, the tubing unrolls nicely to fit snugly against the inside of the bucket and requires only small amounts of hot glue in a few spots.

Left: The material used to create this pattern is a large piece of perforated aluminum sheet metal, which is thinner than the rubber doormat used for the doormat lantern project (see p 113). The ice edges reflect the light beautifully, but this lantern's shallow pattern will disappear quickly if brought indoors.
— Photo by Jennifer Shea Hedberg

ICE APPLIQUÉ LANTERN

ICE SNOWBALL LANTERN

DOORMAT ICE LANTERN

PLASTIC TUBE ICE LANTERN

TIP

WHITE ICE
Mineral-rich water saved from making the globe ice lantern was used to create this more opaque rabbit appliqué.

Ice Appliqué Lantern

There are many ways to make small shapes of ice to attach to ice lanterns. Cookie cutters as well as candy and soap molds are great options as they're made of materials that will hold up to temperature changes. Basic shapes with crisp edges are best for this clear-ice-on-clear-ice application. I've chosen to use metal cookie cutters with open tops for this project since they're commonly found in most kitchens and thrift shops. I've opted to use a globe ice lantern since its round shape makes adding an appliqué a little more challenging than with a flat-sided ice lantern.

WHAT YOU NEED

Globe ice lantern

Cookie cutters

Baking pan

Scissors

Screwdriver

Hammer

Floating candle and matches
or
LED lights

1 GLOBE ICE LANTERN

Drilled chimney for candle use

STEP 1: Make a small globe ice lantern according to directions on page 29. Place the lantern with the large opening facing down. If you plan to use a candle, create a chimney with a power drill and spade bit (1-1.5"). Set aside on a piece of plastic in below-freezing temps until ready to apply ice shapes.

2 COOKIE CUTTERS

STEP 2: Choose the cookie cutter shapes you'd like to try and put them in a baking pan. Consider trying several different shapes as one might work better than another. Add enough water to fill the pan and all the cookie cutters.

3 LAY FLAT

4 FREEZE

5 RELEASE

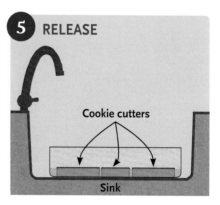

Cookie cutters

Sink

STEP 3: Lay the baking pan filled with water and cookie cutters flat on a metal, stone or glass outdoors (if temps are below freezing) or in a freezer.

Do not lay the pan on snow: You want the ice to freeze all the way through.

STEP 4: Allow the water in the pan to freeze solid. It should take about 6 hours depending on how cold it is outdoors or in your freezer.

STEP 5: Put the pan filled with cookie cutters and ice in the sink. Allow it to sit for a few minutes until the ice loosens from the pan. (Resist the urge to run warm water over the bottom of the pan as it could crack the ice.) Remove the ice from the pan.

6 REMOVE EXTRA ICE

7 REFREEZE

8 RELEASE

STEP 6: Put the rectangle of ice on a cutting board and use a screwdriver and hammer to gently break up the ice outside the cookie cutters. Remove as much of the extra ice as possible.

STEP 7: Return the cookie cutters with ice inside to the pan. Put the pan back into freezing temps for 30 minutes or so to refreeze any cracks or fissures in the ice.

STEP 8: Put the baking pan with the cookie cutters back into the sink right side up and allow it to sit for 5 minutes. The ice should slip out of the cookie cutters.

A pink-hearted appliqué ice lantern created by Mary Arneson shines for Valentine's Day.
— Photo by Stephen L. Garrett

9 KEEP FROZEN

STEP 9: Put the ice cookies in individual plastic bags and then back in the freezer to get really cold!

10 FLATTEN ONE SIDE

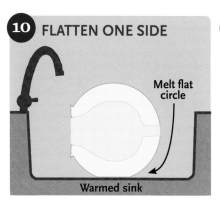

Melt flat circle

Warmed sink

STEP 10: The globe ice lantern is round and the ice cookie is flat, so it's necessary to flatten one side of the globe before the two can be frozen together. Run warm water in a sink and let the water go down the drain. Put the lantern on its side so the warmed sink can melt a flat circle into one side of the ice.

11 APPLY ICE COOKIE

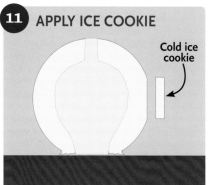

Cold ice cookie

STEP 11: Take an ice cookie out of the freezer (it should be very cold) and stick the flat side of the cookie to the freshly flattened side of the globe ice lantern. Hold the ice cookie in place until it sticks.

Put the ice lantern with the ice appliqué in a plastic bag and back into freezing temps until ready to display.

12 LIGHT THE ICE APPLIQUÉ LANTERN

See pages 31 and 52 for globe ice lantern lighting instructions.

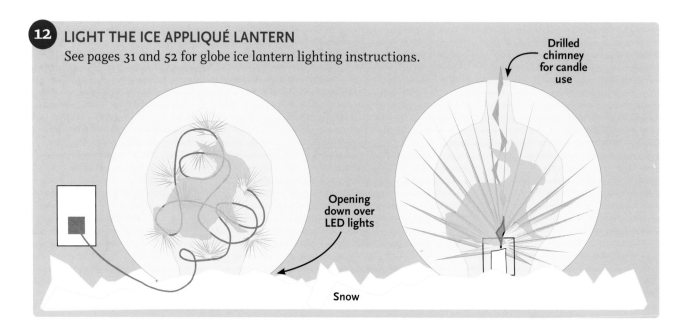

Drilled chimney for candle use

Opening down over LED lights

Snow

*This charming ice lantern was
made by Mary Arneson, who
glued a Christmas tree-shaped
ice cookie to an ice lantern made
from a 4-sided container.*
— *Photo by Stephen L. Garrett*

Ice snowball lanterns light up the dark at Midwinter Light, an annual event in The Commons park near U.S. Bank Stadium in downtown Minneapolis.
— *Photo by Elizabeth Shea Hedberg*

✳ Ice Snowball ✳✳ Lantern

"Nothing worthwhile in life comes easily." — *Hamilton Holt*

Keep this adage in mind while working on this project, which requires the gluing of many ice cubes to the surface of an ice lantern. My friend and fellow ice artist Mary Arneson was inspired to create an ice lantern like this when she saw an Araré Teapot at Mia (Minneapolis Institute of Art). The raised dot pattern created a pleasing visual texture which Mary duplicated in ice. Her creation moved me to experiment with irregularly shaped ice cubes arranged for a more haphazard, organic look. Either way, gluing ice to ice requires flat surfaces, water and cold temps of 8°F or colder. If very cold temps aren't available, use a limited application of "snice" (snow mixed with water, p 43). The resulting ice lantern lit from within will be a show-stopper!

WHAT YOU NEED	

Large globe ice lantern

Large bag of ice cubes
in any shape

Cold water

Cold temps
or deep freezer

Clothes Iron

Tight-fitting nitrile
or latex gloves

Hair dryer

Candle
in candle holder

Matches

① GLOBE ICE LANTERN

Thin ice shell

② ICE CUBES

Bag of ice cubes

STEP 1: Make a large globe ice lantern with a thin shell according to directions on page 29. Place the large opening facing down and drill a chimney through the top with a drill and spade bit *(see p 54)*. Set it aside on a piece of plastic in below-freezing temps (8°F or colder, if possible).

STEP 2: Pour the ice cubes into containers with open tops to make them easy to reach. Keep them in below-freezing temps.

Close-up of Mary Arneson's "Araré" ice lantern (right)
— Photo by Dale Hammerschmidt

3 WORK SPACE

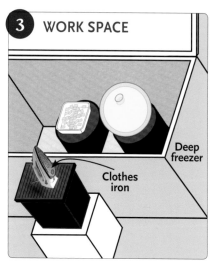

Deep freezer

Clothes iron

STEP 3: Consider where you are going to glue the ice cubes to the ice lantern. Choose somewhere cold with access to an electrical outlet.

MY SET-UP: I put an up-side-down bucket in a large chest freezer and then place the globe ice lantern on top of the bucket with the chimney hole facing up. (This allows me to work comfortably with the freezer top open and to occasionally close the lid to let the ice cubes freeze into place.) I put the ice cubes into a plastic container also in the freezer. My iron is plugged in near the freezer and sits with the warm surface toward me on a catch basin (see Tools and Supplies, p 12).

4 GLUE

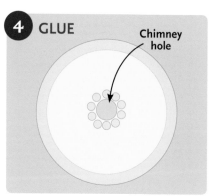

Chimney hole

STEP 4: Start gluing ice cubes around the chimney hole at the top of the globe ice lantern.

TO GLUE:

Ⓐ Hold an ice cube in your dominant hand with the side you're going to glue facing up.

Tight fitting nitrile or latex gloves work well to hold slippery little pieces of ice.

Ⓑ Swipe the ice cube against the warm iron so that the ice surface becomes flat and wet.

Ⓒ Place the ice cube's flat, wet surface on the cold globe ice lantern.

Ⓓ Hold in place (as still as possible) for a few seconds until the ice cube sticks to the globe.

5 KEEP GLUING

STEP 5: Keep gluing ice cubes in the gaps between the secured ice cubes, going around and around.

6 KEEP GLUING!

STEP 6: As you're working, try not to get caught up in placing the ice cubes perfectly. Just keep gluing the cubes into the gaps until you've reached the halfway point. Let the ice globe set for at least 1 hour in below-freezing temps.

7 FLIP OVER

8 KEEP GLUING — Large opening up

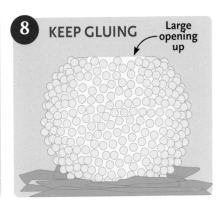

9 FUSE ICE

Towel in plastic bag as cushion

STEP 7: After the ice cubes have had a chance to set, flip the ice globe over and carefully place it on a plastic bag with a towel inside. (The goal is to provide a soft nest for the lantern that doesn't stick to the ice.)

STEP 8: Start where you left off and work up. Keep gluing the ice cubes until you reach the lantern's large flat opening. Let the globe sit for at least 1 hour in freezing temps.

STEP 9: With a hair dryer, blow heated air over the entire lantern to solidify the union of ice and ice cubes. Let the ice lantern sit again in below-freezing temps for at least one hour.

10 LIGHT IT UP!

STEP 10: Flip the ice snowball lantern over so that the chimney hole is up and position it over a candle to light it up.

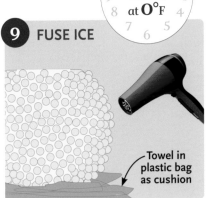

This sparkling orb gleams with hundreds of bullet-shaped ice cubes glued onto an ice lantern with a chimney drilled in the round top. Thin-shelled ice lanterns allow candlelight to shine through many layers of ice.
— Photo by Jennifer Shea Hedberg

*Ice lanterns with a textured
surface are best displayed in cold weather
as warm temps can cause the pattern
to lose definition quickly.
— Photo by Jennifer Shea Hedberg*

✳ Doormat
Ice Lantern

Any 3-dimensional sheet of non-porous material can be used to line a bucket. When the bucket is filled with water and allowed to partially freeze (see p 19), the ice surface will reveal patterned indentations once it's pulled free from the liner. One of the best 3-D liners is a rubber doormat because it's thick, waterproof, flexible and comes in a multitude of sizes and designs.

To help illustrate, I made the large bucket see-through and pink.

1 WRAP

2 FILL

STEP 1: Wrap a 24" x 36" rubber doormat inside a 6-gallon utility bucket (found at brewery supply stores). Squeezing the corners together at the floor of the bucket will make it stand tall and fit perfectly.

STEP 2: Put the bucket where it can freeze (outdoors in below-freezing temps or in a freezer) on snow, frozen ground or some form of insulation. (The water in the bottom of the bucket must remain unfrozen.) Fill the bucket until the water reaches 2" below the top.

3 FREEZE

STEP 3: Freeze for around 30 hours or until a thick crust of ice has formed inside the bucket. Look down through the top to see how thick the ice crust has become. Let it freeze until the ice is around 3" thick.

4 THAW

STEP 4: Put the bucket in a sink or bathtub and let the ice thaw for 15-30 minutes. Eventually, the ice will slide out of the bucket.

5 POUR

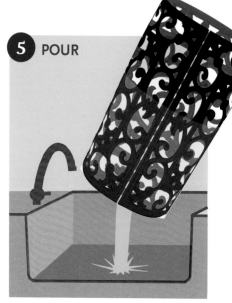

STEP 5: Slide the ice out of the bucket to release the water from the lantern's unfrozen bottom. (Any ice that has formed can easily be broken.)

6 PEEL

STEP 6: Peel away the doormat to reveal indentations in the ice. If extra ice has enveloped the doormat in spots, remove it with a scraper or wood chisel. Continue to peel the mat free from the lantern.

7 STORE

STEP 7: Place the ice lantern in a plastic bag and store it in below-freezing temps until ready to display.

8 LIGHT

8 ALT: LED LIGHTS

8 ALT: CREATE CHIMNEY

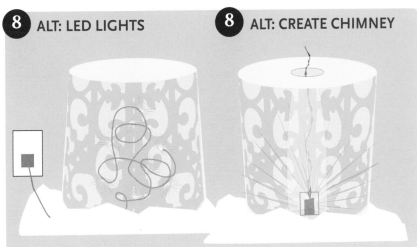

STEP 8: When you're ready to display the ice lantern, position it with the large opening facing up. Place a candle in the bottom of the lantern — floating candles work best.

ALT STEP 8: Fill the cavity of the ice lantern with a string of LED lights intended for outdoor use. Place the lantern on the ground in the desired location and turn on the lights.

ALT STEP 8: The magic of a candle, the beauty of the ice and better wind protection make drilling a chimney a great alternative. (For chimney drilling instructions, see p 54.)

Overlap the plastic tubing in spots for an even more dramatic effect. The only caveat is that it may make removing the tubing a little more challenging.
— Photo by Jennifer Shea Hedberg

Plastic Tube Ice Lantern

Using plastic tubing to create texture in ice works very well because it's non-porous and is naturally curved like the inside of the bucket. It's easy to hold in place with hot glue. Once the ice has frozen and the tubes are removed, the lines created in the ice will be deep and convoluted.

To help illustrate, I made the large bucket see-through.

1 HOT GLUE

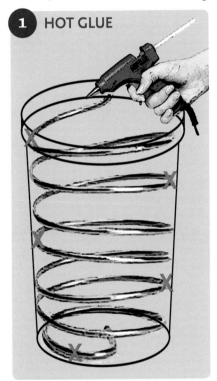

2 FILL

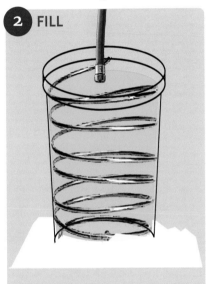

STEP 1: Starting at the bottom of the bucket, attach a coil of plastic tubing to the inside of a 7-gallon utility bucket. Use as little hot glue as possible to facilitate eventual removal of the ice.

X's mark the few places where the tube should be glued.

STEP 2: Put the bucket where you plan to freeze it (outdoors in below-freezing temps or in a freezer) on snow, frozen ground or some form of insulation. Fill it with water until the water reaches 2" below the top.

WHAT YOU NEED

7-gallon
utility bucket

20 ft of 1/4"
plastic tubing

Hot glue gun
and hot glue

Tap water

Cold temps
or deep freezer

Candle
in candle holder

Matches

— OPTIONAL —

Wood chisel

3 FREEZE

30 HOURS at 0°F

STEP 3: Freeze for around 30 hours or until a thick crust of ice has formed inside the bucket. This is a longer freezing time than for other bucket ice lanterns because the project uses a larger bucket and more water.

Look down through the top of the ice to see how thick the ice crust has become. Let it freeze until the ice is around 3" thick.

4 THAW AND RELEASE

STEP 4: Put the bucket upside down in a sink or bathtub and let it thaw for 15-30 minutes. After this period, the ice may slide out of the bucket.

If the ice doesn't easily release, the hot glue may have anchored it to the bucket. To remedy, remove any exposed glue and, with the bucket facing down, twist sharply from side to side. Repeat until the ice slides out of the bucket.

5 POUR

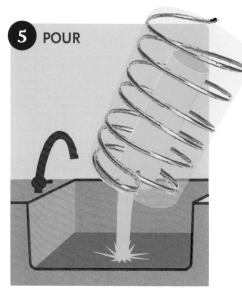

STEP 5: The bottom of the ice lantern (where it was sitting in the snow) should be unfrozen (or easily broken) so that the water pours out easily.

6 PEEL

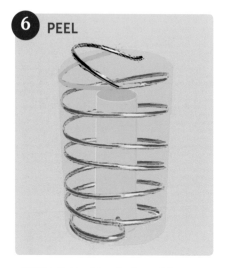

STEP 6: Peel back the rubber plastic tubing to reveal the indentations left in the ice. If necessary, use a scraper or wood chisel to release the tubing from the ice.

7 LIGHT

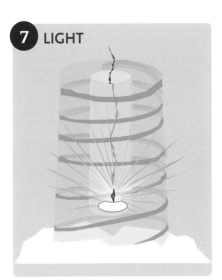

STEP 7: When you're ready to display the ice lantern, position it with the opening facing up. Place a floating candle inside the lantern.

7 ALT: LED LIGHTS AND CREATE CHIMNEY

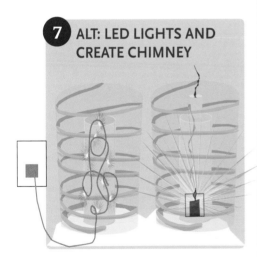

ALT STEP 7: Turn the lantern open side down and fill the cavity with a string of LED lights intended for outdoor use. Or drill a chimney for a candle. (Chimney instructions, see p 54.)

Right: This is a close-up of another ice lantern textured with plastic tubing. I love the undulating loops of light.

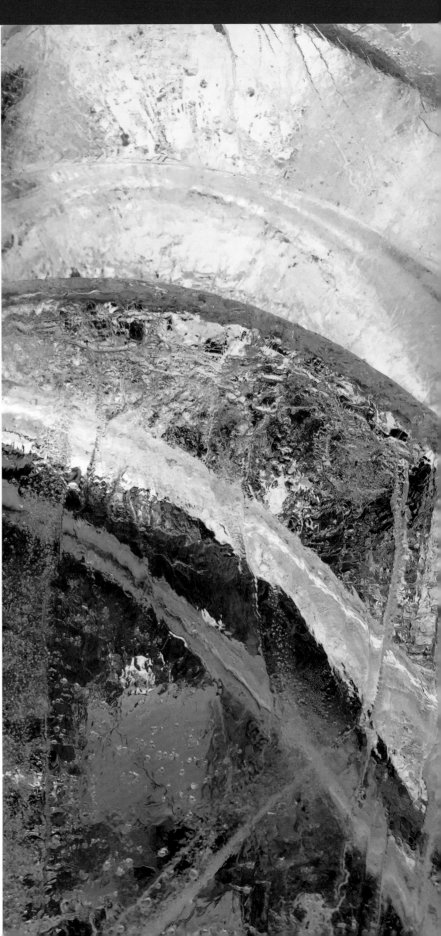

Overlapping strips and pieces of crepe paper can add vibrant, glowing color to ice lanterns using the balloon pressure method (see p 145).
— **Photo by Jennifer Shea Hedberg**

Freezing Objects into Ice

When adding items to ice, it's important to know how they'll interact with water. Some things float; others sink. Once you determine whether the item you want to add will do one or the other, you can choose a strategy for freezing it into ice.

A FEW THINGS TO CONSIDER:

Float (Bottom Up)

When I make a *Floral Bucket Ice Lantern (see p 123)*, I like the flowers to look as though they're growing up from the bottom of the ice lantern. Hot glue holds flowers to the floor of a utility bucket. When water is added to the bucket, the flowers float up — standing tall while the ice freezes around them.

Float (Top Down)

If you want to add floating items from the top of a container, such as with the *Floral Globe Ice Lantern (see p 127)*, and you want those items to stay submerged and in position, a combination of wire and hot glue works well.

Float (Using Weights)

A floating item can also be kept in place by attaching it to a weight, as seen in the *Crepe Paper Ice Lantern (see p 139)*. The weight keeps one end of the object down while the other end floats up.

Balloon Pressure Method

The technique for creating the *Leaves in Globe Ice Lantern (see p 145)* starts with a crust of ice. Once items are added, an air-filled balloon holds them against the ice while a new layer of ice freezes them into place.

Food Color Solution

Food color doesn't work well with the partial-freeze method *(see p 19)*. But capturing color in an ice cube first changes everything. Check out the *Food Color Ice Cube Lantern (see p 151)* to see how well this discovery works.

Adding Voids

Adding 3-D objects that can be removed after the ice has formed around them creates voids in the ice. The *Finnish Glass Ice Lantern (see p 157)* uses this concept to create chains of beautiful bubbles in the ice.

FLORAL BUCKET ICE LANTERN

FLORAL GLOBE ICE LANTERN

CREPE PAPER ICE LANTERN

LEAVES IN GLOBE ICE LANTERN

FOOD COLOR ICE CUBE LANTERN

FINNISH GLASS ICE LANTERN

This floral bucket ice lantern photo holds a very special place in my heart. Growing within the ice are flowers that I picked from my mother's wild flower garden the year she died.
— Photo by Jennifer Shea Hedberg

✳ Floral Bucket
✳✳ Ice Lantern

*Flowers are like ice in that they are both beautiful and ephemeral.
I can't think of anything better than to marry the two. If your garden fades
away come winter, use a freezer to capture it at its peak and bring out the
bottled sunshine on a cold winter's day.*

To help illustrate, I made the bucket see-through.

1 FLOWER ARRANGING

Waterline

12"

X

Focal
point

STEP 1: Sort your flowers into 3 small arrangements that will fit in
the 12" from the bucket floor to the waterline (2" below the top of the
bucket). Keep in mind that the focal point tends to be in the center.

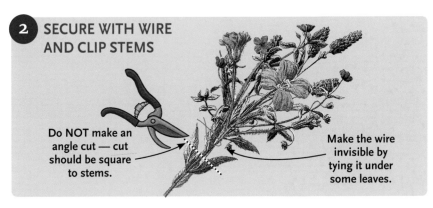

**2 SECURE WITH WIRE
AND CLIP STEMS**

Do NOT make an
angle cut — cut
should be square
to stems.

Make the wire
invisible by
tying it under
some leaves.

STEP 2: Secure each bundle with a short piece of wire and hide the
ends of the wire by tucking them behind or into the leaves. Flat-cut the
stems of the bundle where they will touch the floor of the bucket.

WHAT YOU NEED

Heavy-duty
5-gallon utility bucket
and bucket lid

9-12 flowers
and flower clippers

Thin wire
and wire clippers

Baking paper

Hot glue gun
and hot glue sticks

2-3 thin bottles
filled with liquid

Cold tap water

Cold temps
or deep freezer

LED lights

3 HOT GLUE AND FLOWERS

Baking paper

Hot glue is clear, so to help illustrate I made it hot pink!

STEP 3: With your floral bundles standing by, create a small pool of hot glue on a sheet of baking paper.

Quickly push the flat end of one of the bundles into the hot glue pool and hold it straight until the hot glue is hard.

Add more hot glue to the base of the bundle, if needed.

Repeat this gluing process with all flower bundles.

TIP

KEEP IT STEADY
Use a few liquid-filled bottles to prop up and hold the floral bundles straight and steady while the glue is hardening.

4 MORE HOT GLUE

STEP 4: Peel the baking paper from the hardened glue base of one floral bundle. Add a small amount of hot glue to the base's flat underside. Quickly press the bundle onto the floor of the bucket, holding it in place until steady. Repeat this gluing process for all flower bundles.

TIP

FLOWER IN ICE

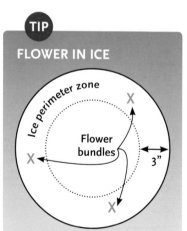

Ice perimeter zone

Flower bundles

3"

The floor of the bucket has a diameter of 10". Making the ice lantern walls 3" thick will insure that the perimeter ice can contain your flower bundles. It's best if the flowers and leaves are positioned so they are close to, but not touching, the bucket sides.

5 ADD WATER

STEP 5: Place the prepared bucket on snow, frozen ground or insulation in freezing temps. Put the end of a garden hose into the bucket until it reaches the floor. Turn on the water so that it flows gently into the bucket. (No garden hose? Bring water to the bucket, but pour gently.)

24 HOURS at 0°F

6 FREEZE

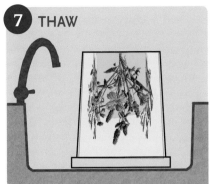

Bucket Lid

STEP 6: Depending on the temperature, the lantern will take anywhere from 12 hours to 3 days to freeze. After the first 24 hours, check every 6 hours or so.

Optional: Put a bucket lid or insulation on top of the bucket while freezing to keep the top ice from getting too thick. This will also make it easier to see how thick the ice is becoming.

7 THAW

STEP 7: Flip the bucket upside-down in a sink and allow it to thaw for 15-30 minutes. The ice will fall out of the bucket. To cushion any impact, place a plastic bag with a towel inside between the ice and the sink.

If you discover the flowers have not frozen sufficiently into the ice, add fresh water and let it continue to freeze. This will help make the ice clearer, too!

Don't let the ice freeze solid!

8 POUR

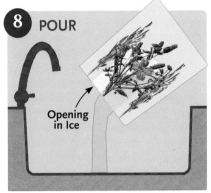

Opening in Ice

STEP 8: Release the water from the hole in the lantern's unfrozen bottom. Any ice that has formed there can be easily chipped open using a knife or a screwdriver.

9 LIGHT

STEP 9: When you're ready to display the ice lantern, place it over LED lights or position the ice lantern in the sunlight and enjoy the glow!

You can use a candle, too. Drill a chimney, and cut back any interior stems that might be within reach of the flame.

This floral globe ice lantern features
ordinary grocery-store flowers frozen in midwinter.
— Photo by Jana Freiband

Floral Globe Ice Lantern

Friends sometimes ask whether it's possible to freeze objects into the ice of a globe ice lantern. In the past I've suggested adding cranberries, glitter and food color since these items can be forced down the neck of a balloon. But cranberries and glitter float to the top and most of the food color is flushed out with the unfrozen water. Then I discovered a better way: Use an up- side-down globe ice lantern as the mold, add the flowers through the open- ing in the ice and continue the freezing process upside down. This project is rewarding but the process can be challenging. **Read through all the instruc- tions before you begin. Then make sure to prepare the following items and have them ready to use for the assembly phase.**

A. Tin Can Bases

This project calls for flipping a globe ice lantern upside down to stuff it with flowers. Its round top (now the bottom) needs a stable cold base while you work with it. A tin can with the top and bottom removed will do the trick. It's strong, will hold a spherical form and conducts the cold.

A1 LIDS OFF

STEP A1: Remove the tops and bottoms of two 15 oz food cans.

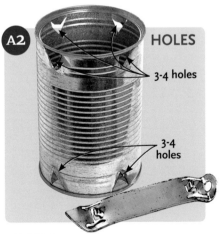

A2 HOLES

3-4 holes

3-4 holes

STEP A2: With a can tapper, create 3-4 triangular shaped holes in the sides of both cans. The tin cans must be cold or they will melt grooves into the ice, so keep them in the freezer.

B. Weighted Insert

A rock-filled container has two important jobs — to keep the flowers down and to help create a hollow space in the ice globe for a candle.

Punched holes

Long fireplace match sticks

STEP B1: Punch 4 holes .5" down from top edge of a 32 oz plastic to-go container. The holes should be directly across from each other.

STEP B2: Fill with small stones up to 1" below the top of the container.

STEP B3: Using strong scissors, cut the heads from 2 long (11") fireplace matches and push them through the holes in the plastic container. Put one matchstick in the North hole and out the South hole. Put the other matchstick in the East hole, under or over the first matchstick, and out the West hole.

C. Insulating Bag

After the flowers have been added, you'll need a plastic bag filled with packing peanuts to nicely insulate the ice lantern opening while the flowers freeze into the ice.

STEP C1: Fill a plastic shopping bag with about 4 cups of packing peanuts (Styrofoam pellets).

STEP C2: Secure the bag with a twist-tie.

D. Floral Bundles

Prep and bundle the flowers before you begin the assembly process. Smaller, simpler bunches of highly colorful and translucent blossoms work best in ice lanterns. White blossoms can't be seen as well as a red rose. One rose, one stem of a filler flower (Limonium), and some greens is perfect. That's it. Too many flowers in the globe will look cramped and may get mashed up against the inside of the ice.

D1 FLOWER ARRANGING

8"

X

Focal point

STEP D1: Sort your flowers and create 3 small arrangements (2-3 flower stems and 1 stem of greens) that will fit inside a large globe ice lantern. The focal point will be about 4" from the blossom tops.

Note: The above illustration shows the flowers upside down as they will be placed in the globe for freezing.

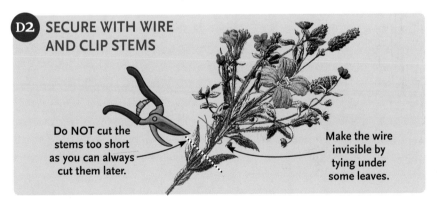

D2 SECURE WITH WIRE AND CLIP STEMS

Do NOT cut the stems too short as you can always cut them later.

Make the wire invisible by tying under some leaves.

STEP D2: Secure each floral bundle tightly with a short piece of wire and tuck the ends behind a leaf. Make fresh cuts in the stems at a 90° angle and put them in water-filled vases until ready to use.

E. Globe Ice Lantern

For this project, the initial globe of ice should be about .75" thick — thin, but strong enough to keep its shape and not leak. These instructions for making a globe ice lantern differ from those found on page 29.

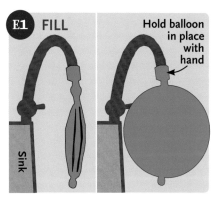

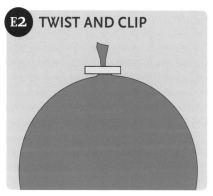

STEP E1: Fill a globe ice lantern balloon with cold tap water by stretching the balloon's mouth around the water faucet head to form a seal. Hold the balloon tightly in place with thumb and forefinger as it fills with water to desired size.

STEP E2: Twist the neck of the balloon and seal it with an easy-close balloon clip.

Note: Do not tie the balloon as you will need to open it again before the freezing process begins.

12 HOURS at 0°F

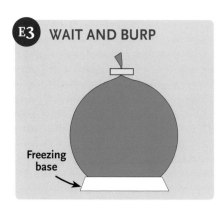

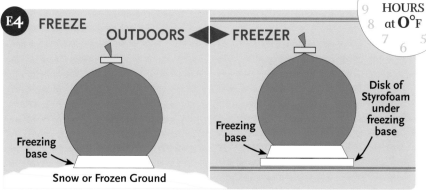

STEP E3: Let the water-filled balloon sit at above-freezing temps for at least 6 hours, or overnight, then undo the clip and release any air that has risen to the top. Reclip the balloon.

Warning! Failure to do this step will weaken the top of the ice lantern, causing water leakage in the assembly phase.

STEP E4: Place the water-filled balloon and freezing base directly on the frozen ground or snow to keep the bottom of the ice globe from freezing.

Let it freeze for 12 hours at 0°F — longer if warmer and shorter if colder.

ALT STEP E4: Place the water-filled balloon and freezing base on a piece of Styrofoam in a freezer.

Let it freeze for 12 hours at 0°F — longer if warmer and shorter if colder.

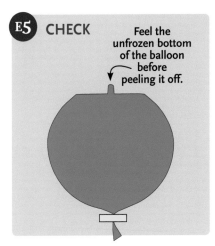

Feel the unfrozen bottom of the balloon before peeling it off.

Assemble the Lantern

This project entails freezing an ice globe, filling it with flowers, and freezing it again. It's crucial to move through the assembly steps quickly, so be sure to prepare all needed items before you begin. The tin cans should be cold. The flower bundles should be gathered. The weighted insert and the bag of packing peanuts for insulation should be ready.

STEP E5: Give the water in the balloon time to freeze. The ice crust must be about .75" thick.

Check the thickness of the ice by pressing firmly on the balloon while it sits in the freezing base. If the ice cracks or breaks from the pressure, let it freeze for another 6 hours and recheck.

If the ice feels solid, lift the balloon off the freezing base and turn it upside down. Find the tiny rubber bump that protrudes from the balloon's flat unfrozen bottom. Push your forefinger into the bump so you can pinch the ice between your thumb and forefinger to determine its thickness.

If the ice is about .75" thick, it's ready for the assembly phase.

Check the thickness of the ice before opening the balloon!

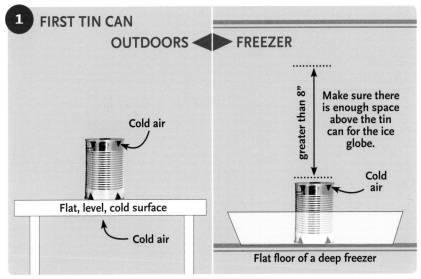

1 FIRST TIN CAN

OUTDOORS ◀▶ FREEZER

Cold air

Flat, level, cold surface

Cold air

greater than 8"

Make sure there is enough space above the tin can for the ice globe.

Cold air

Flat floor of a deep freezer

STEP 1: Take one of the tin cans out of the freezer and place it, with the open ends facing up and down, in the location where you'll freeze the ice globe for the second time. This tin can will be used in Step 8.

If outdoors (in below-freezing temps), place the tin can on a flat, stable, level cold surface, like a glass tabletop or stonework.

If using a freezer, put down a large plastic flat-bottomed container on a flat surface in the freezer. (This is insurance in case the ice breaks, so make sure the container is large enough to hold all the water you add.) Place the tin can in the middle of the plastic container in the freezer and take note of the space above it. Will there be enough room for the ice globe?

TIP

CHECK UPSIDE DOWN
In case the balloon breaks while you're checking the thickness of the ice, keep the balloon upside down. The water will stay in the ice and you can let it continue to freeze.

2 SECOND TIN CAN

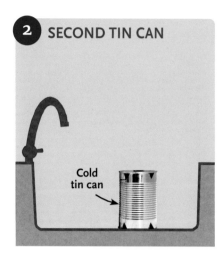

Cold tin can

STEP 2: Take the second tin can out of the freezer and place it in a sink.

3 UPSIDE-DOWN BALLOON

Unfrozen bottom

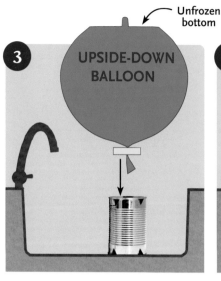

STEP 3: Place the globe ice lantern balloon **upside down** on the tin can. Make sure it's balanced and the unfrozen bottom is straight up.

4 PEEL BALLOON

STEP 4: Slice open the balloon with a pair of scissors or knife and peel the rubber so it hangs down around the tin can.

5 REMOVE WATER

STEP 5: Remove about 3-4 soup ladles of water. The globe should be 1/2-3/4 full of water.

Why? It's easier to add the flowers when there is less water and also easier to carry the lantern.

6 ADD FLOWERS

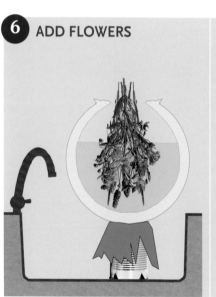

ADD TOYS, TOO!
See page 137 for instructions and return to Step 6 to continue.

STEP 6: Hold all three flower bunches in your hands and gently squeeze them together as you guide them into the open hole of the ice globe. Protect the blossoms and keep the stems from bending as they enter the water. Arrange so the desired flowers face outward.

7 ADD WEIGHTED INSERT

STEP 7: Separate the flower stems and lower the weighted insert in between the branches until the matchsticks rest on top of the ice.

Double-check the floral bundles to make sure you like the look. If you lift the weighted insert to adjust the flowers, make sure you recheck the flower positioning when you lower it again.

Thin globe ice lantern shells make it easy to see flowers through the ice and rearrange before freezing the globe for the second time.

8 BALANCE ON TIN CAN

Cold tin can

9 ADD WATER

10 INSULATE TOP

Bag of Styrofoam peanuts provides insulation.

STEP 8: Carefully lift the globe and its contents and place it on the tin can previously positioned in the freezing location. Discard the broken balloon.

Adjust the ice globe on the tin can so that the opening in the ice is straight up and the water-line looks level.

Warning! Make sure that the ice globe is balanced and secure before you take your hands away.

STEP 9: Place the end of a funnel in an opening between the ice, the flowers and the weighted insert. Slowly pour distilled water into the funnel until the water level in the globe is approximately 1" below the top of the ice.

Why? Water expands as it freezes and we want the globe's top to freeze last. If there is too much water in the globe, it will be pushed out the top and deposit streaks of white, hazy ice on the outside of the globe.

Warning! Don't put any water in the weighted insert.

STEP 10: Position the bag of packing peanuts on top of the weighted insert and the opening in the ice.

Why? The flowers' protruding stems make it difficult to insulate the top of the ice globe. We want this area to freeze last, so it must stay warmer than the rest of the globe. The plastic bag filled with packing peanuts will form itself around the stems and serve as an insulated cover for the globe's opening.

11 FREEZE AGAIN AND CHECK OFTEN!

12 HOURS at 10°F

STEP 11: Freeze the globe until the flowers are mostly encased in ice. The lantern's walls should be approximately 2"-3" thick and its internal cavity at least the size of your fist. Depending on temps, freezing the lantern could take 12-48 hours, but it's important to check its progress regularly.

In temps of 10°F to 20°F, check the first time after 12 hours by lifting the packing peanut bag and pulling out the weighted insert. Look to see if the flowers are incorporated into the ice of the lantern's walls. If more freezing time is needed, replace the weighted insert and the packing peanut bag and check again in 4-6 hours.

Once the ice has a grip on the flowers, it's not necessary to replace the stone-filled insert. Just add more distilled water, replace the bag of packing peanuts and continue freezing until the flowers are secure.

Do not freeze solid! *Be sure to leave enough room for a light source.*

12 POUR

STEP 12: When the flowers are nicely frozen into the ice, remove the insulating bag and the weighted insert and tip the lantern over to pour out any remaining water.

13 CUT STEMS

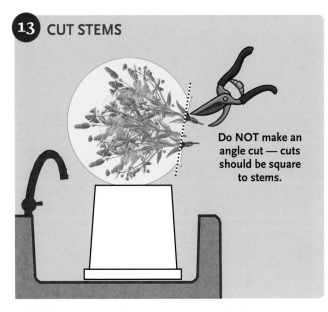

Do NOT make an angle cut — cuts should be square to stems.

STEP 13: Turn a plastic bucket upside down in a sink. Place the ice lantern gently on its side on top of the bucket. Use clippers to trim wires and stems as close to the ice as possible.

Put the finished floral globe ice lantern in a plastic bag and keep it in below-freezing temps until ready to display.

14 LIGHT IT UP!

STEP 14: When you're ready to display the ice lantern, pop it over some LED lights or place it in the sunlight and enjoy the glow!

To illuminate the lantern with a candle, drill a chimney *(see p 54)* and trim away any foliage that might be in the path of the candle's heat.

TIP

IRON MINERAL LINES
If too much water was left in the ice globe during the second freezing phase, lines of white ice can drip down the outside of the ice globe. A clothes iron (non-steam setting) can melt the lines away, but keep the iron moving to avoid creating flat spots on the globe.

FUN IDEA: A Halloween-themed globe looks especially spooky with the mineral lines intact.

WARNING! Using electrical appliances around water can be dangerous.

— *Photo by Jennifer Shea Hedberg*

ADD 3-D ITEMS TO GLOBES

Adding toy figures or other water-resistant 3-D objects to a globe ice lantern is incredibly fun. The objects will be upside down while freezing and will probably float, so it's necessary to hold them in position with a length of stiff wire and hot glue.

A WIRE

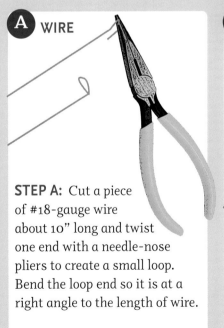

STEP A: Cut a piece of #18-gauge wire about 10" long and twist one end with a needle-nose pliers to create a small loop. Bend the loop end so it is at a right angle to the length of wire.

B HOT GLUE

STEP B: Put a dab of hot glue on the bottom of the object you want to add to the ice and push the loop of the wire into the glue. Reinforce with another dab of glue. Let the hot glue cool.

C ADD TO FLOWERS

STEP C: Add the figure to a floral bundle and secure it with a small piece of thin wire.

D CONTINUE WITH ASSEMBLY See Step 6 of the assembly directions, page 132.

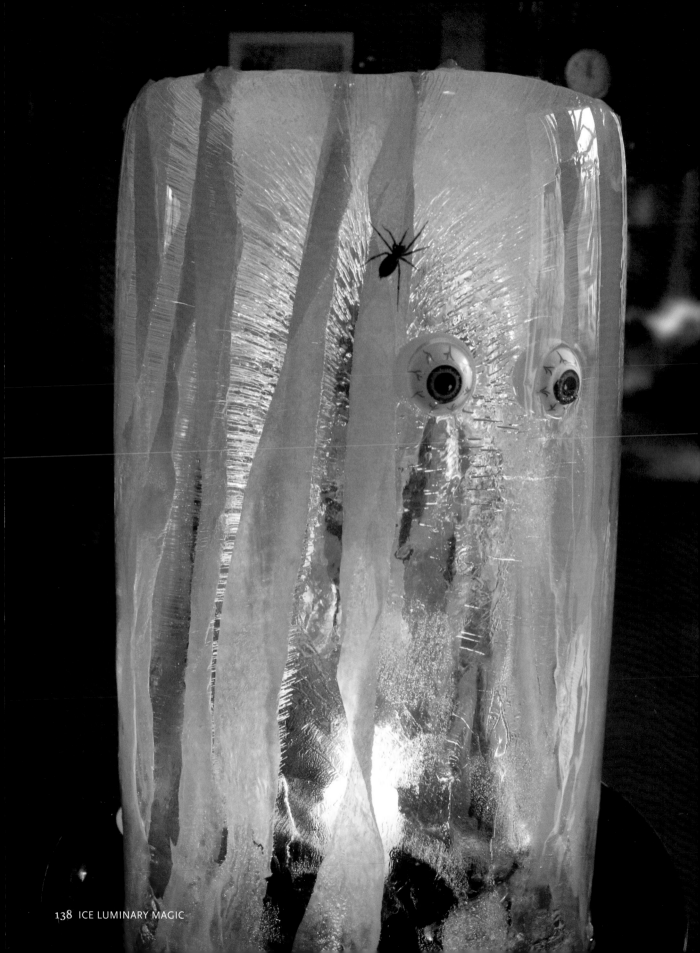

Crepe Paper Ice Lantern

Incorporating crepe paper, tissue paper or other types of material into a bucket ice lantern using weights is an easy way to add wild color. The resulting ice lantern can be lit with candles or with colored LED lights for even more pizzazz.

To help illustrate, I made the bucket see-through.

1 CUT

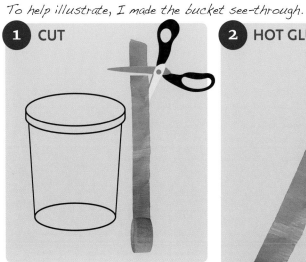

2 HOT GLUE

STEP 1: Cut several long strips of crepe paper so they are a few inches longer than the height of your bucket.

STEP 2: Hot glue a quarter to one end of a strip of crepe paper and a penny to the other end. Repeat for all pieces of crepe paper.

Left: While I set up this crepe paper ice lantern, a big fat spider lowered itself down from the ceiling onto the ice. The spider seemed so stunned by the cold that I started snapping photos. If you like the spooky look and don't want to rely on serendipity, use a plastic spider. You can freeze it into an ice lantern by gluing it onto the bucket wall with its legs facing toward the center of the bucket before adding water.
— Photo by Jennifer Shea Hedberg

WHAT YOU NEED

Heavy-duty
utility bucket

Crepe paper
or tissue paper

12 quarters
and 12 pennies

Hot glue
and hot glue gun

Cold tap water

Cold temps
or deep freezer

Candle in candle holder
and matches
or
LED lights

— OPTIONAL —

Ping pong balls
with painted eyes

Small plastic spider

3 ADD PAPER

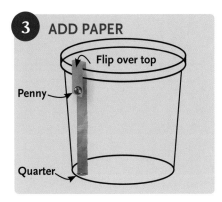

STEP 3: Put the quarter end of one of the crepe paper strips on the floor of the bucket and drape the penny end over the top. Move the quarter end so it is about .5"-1" away from the wall of the bucket. The quarter should be heavy enough to hold one end of the crepe paper strip on the bucket floor when the container is filled with water. The penny should be just heavy enough to keep the other end of the crepe paper in place without pulling up the quarter.

TWIST PAPER

Fun Idea: Twist the crepe paper to get a 3-D effect.

4 ADD MORE PAPER

STEP 4: Repeat with all the crepe paper strips so they're positioned all the way around the floor of the bucket.

5 FILL

STEP 5: Gently fill the bucket with water approximately 2" from the top and place the bucket (with the crepe paper and coins) on snow or frozen ground, making the bucket level. Snow and ground will help keep the water in the bottom of the bucket from freezing.

Quarter moved while filling? Reach in or use a stick to rearrange the quarters so they touch the bucket floor about .5"-1" away from the bucket wall.

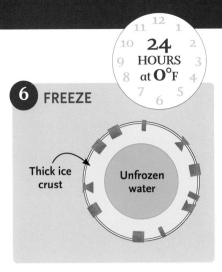

24 HOURS at 0°F

6 FREEZE

Thick ice crust

Unfrozen water

STEP 6: Let the water-filled bucket freeze overnight and check it in the morning. On really cold nights the ice will form in as little as 8-14 hours, but it can take longer when temps are warmer.

Look through the exposed ice on the bucket top to see how thick the walls of ice have become. It's best if the ice walls are 1"-2" thick so that all the crepe paper is encased in ice. The lantern's center core should remain unfrozen.

7 THAW

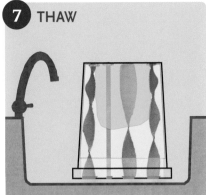

STEP 7: Carry the bucket inside and place it upside down in a sink or bathtub to thaw for about 15-30 minutes.

The ice lantern will release from the bucket and slide into the sink. (A towel in a plastic bag under the bucket will lessen the impact on the sink and ice.) Then lift the bucket off the ice.

After the bucket has been removed, tear off any loose crepe paper and coins.

8 POUR

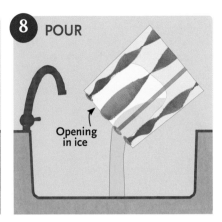

Opening in ice

STEP 8: The bottom of the ice lantern should be unfrozen (or easily broken) so that the water pours out easily.

Below: There are many other items that can be introduced into ice using coins to weigh them down. This bucket ice lantern was created by hot-gluing autumn leaves to fish line and using coins to keep everything in position. The list of embellishments is endless. What will you try?
— Photo by Jennifer Shea Hedberg

9 REMOVE QUARTERS

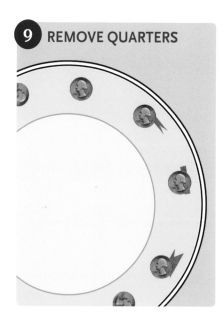

STEP 9: Position the ice lantern so that the end with the quarters faces down in the sink.

Let it sit for 15 minutes. The sink will warm up the quarters and melt the surrounding ice.

Flip the ice lantern over and remove the quarters that have been freed from the ice. Repeat if necessary. Quarters still embedded in the ice can either be left in place or chipped out with a chisel.

10 KEEP FROZEN

STEP 10: Place the ice lantern on or in a plastic bag in below-freezing temps (outdoors or in a freezer) until ready to display.

11 LIGHT IT UP!

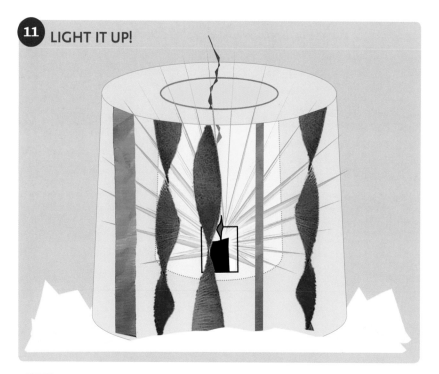

STEP 11: Follow the directions for lighting up a bucket ice lantern with candles or LED lights on page 20. Light and enjoy the glow!

TIP

MORE IDEAS!
Other small floating objects (like the rainbow-colored mylar strips in the lantern shown at right) can be added using this method. Simply weigh down one end of the strip of material with quarters and keep the other end out of the water with pennies.

Why not just hot-glue the mylar to the bottom of the bucket? You can, but the more hot glue you use the more difficult it is to remove the finished ice lantern from the bucket.

*The clear shell of this globe ice lantern reveals
the fine details of the autumn leaves within.*
— Photo by Jennifer Shea Hedberg

Leaves in Globe Ice Lantern

Another way to secure thin objects such as leaves, crepe paper, and tissue paper within an ice lantern is to use the pressure of an air-filled balloon within a shell of ice. It does take a little time and finesse, but the results can be fabulous. For this project, I use a globe ice lantern as the outer shell, which I fill after turning it upside down on its round top. The globe must have a stable base, and a tin can with the top and bottom removed works perfectly. It's strong and conducts the cold.

WHAT YOU NEED

Tin can

Can opener

Can tapper

Globe ice lantern

Real or fake Leaves

12" party balloon

Cold tap water

Cold temps or deep freezer

Candle in candle holder and matches
or
LED lights

1 STABLE BASE

2 HOLES

STEP 1: Remove the top and bottom of a 15 oz tin can.

STEP 2: With a can tapper, create 3-4 triangular shaped holes in the sides of the can. The can must be cold or it will melt grooves into the ice, so keep it in the freezer until ready for use.

3 **GLOBE ICE LANTERN**

Thin-shelled
globe ice lantern

4 **TIN CAN**

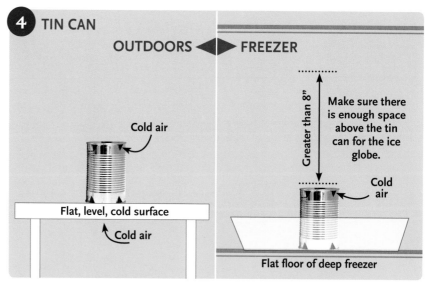

OUTDOORS ◀▶ FREEZER

Cold air

Greater than 8"

Make sure there
is enough space
above the tin
can for the ice
globe.

Cold
air

Flat, level, cold surface

Cold air

Flat floor of deep freezer

STEP 3: Create a thin (.75")
globe ice lantern according to
directions on page 29.

For this lantern, one critical
step is to allow the water-filled
balloon to rest in above-freezing temps for at least 6 hours
after filling. Then undo the clip
and release any air that has ris-
en to the top. Reclip the balloon.

Warning! Failure to release the
air will weaken the ice lantern's
top, causing water leakage
during the assembly phase.

Once you've created a globe ice
lantern with walls about .75"
thick, empty the lantern of all
water. Put the globe in a plastic
bag and store in below-freezing
temps for at least an hour.

1
HOUR
at **0°F**

STEP 4: Take the tin can out of the freezer and place it, with the open
ends facing up and down, in the location where you'll freeze the ice
globe for the second time.

If outdoors (in below-freezing temps), place the tin can on a level,
stable, cold surface like a glass tabletop or stonework.

If using a freezer, put a large plastic flat-bottomed container on a flat
surface in the freezer. (This is insurance in case the ice globe breaks,
so make sure the container is large enough to hold the several cups of
water you'll add to the globe during this phase of the freezing process.) Place the tin can in the middle of the plastic container in the
freezer and take note of the space above it. Will there be enough room
for the ice globe?

5 UPSIDE DOWN

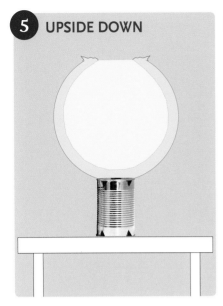

STEP 5: Place the cold and empty globe ice lantern upside down on the cold tin can.

Adjust the ice globe so that the opening in the ice is straight up. Make sure that the ice globe is balanced and secure before you take your hands away.

6 ADD LEAVES

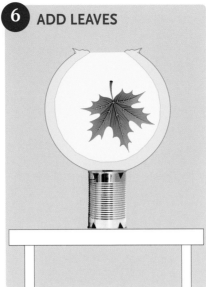

STEP 6: Wet all leaves and position them inside the globe. Remember, the plan is to flip the globe over for display, so look through the ice to make sure the leaves are arranged as you prefer.

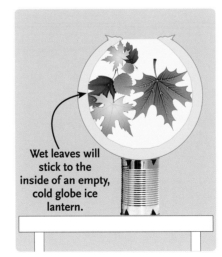

Wet leaves will stick to the inside of an empty, cold globe ice lantern.

7 AIR-FILLED BALLOON

STEP 7: Insert the party balloon into the globe ice lantern and blow it up with air until it's just big enough to keep the leaves pressed against the sides of the globe. Close it with an easy-close clip. *Do not tie the balloon!*

8 ADD WATER

STEP 8: Using a funnel wedged between the air-filled balloon and the inside of the globe, add a small amount of water — just until the water can be seen at the top.

9 FREEZE

3 HOURS at O°F

STEP 9: Let the added water freeze solid. This should take a few hours.

When the new inner layer of ice freezes, it will secure the leaves to the lantern's outer ice shell — as if between two panes of glass.

10 RELEASE AIR / REPEAT

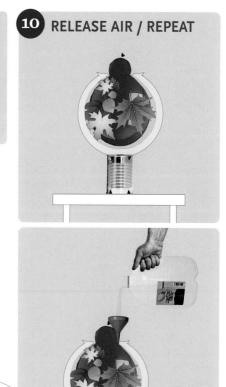

3 HOURS at O°F

STEP 10: Unclip the easy-close clip and release a small amount of air from the balloon. Reclip the balloon. Use the funnel to add more water. Let the added water freeze. Adding and freezing more water will thicken the internal ice layer.

11   REPEAT

STEP 11: Repeat this process until the leaves are secured with at least an additional .5"-1" of ice. If you plan to use a candle, try for thicker walls to ensure the leaves remain secure when the ice walls are thinned by the candle's heat.

Unclip and remove the balloon.

12   REMOVE TIN CAN

STEP 12: Remove the lantern from the tin can and store it in plastic in below-freezing temps until ready for use.

13   LIGHT IT UP!

STEP 13: When you're ready to use the ice lantern, place it over some LED lights or in the sunlight and enjoy the glow as the translucent beauty of the leaves shines through.

13   ALT: LIGHT IT UP!

ALT STEP 13: To light the lantern with a candle, drill a chimney *(see p 54)*. The candlelight will flicker beautifully through the leaves.

Red and blue ice cubes in white
mineral-rich ice make an interesting
Fourth of July decoration
for a dockside evening celebration.
— Photo by Jennifer Shea Hedberg

Food Color Ice Cube Lantern

Adding food color to ice lanterns when using the partial-freeze method is tricky. Since pure water freezes first and pushes impurities toward the lantern's core, most added color is lost when the core's unfrozen water is released. The result is a pale-colored ice lantern. But if the food color is captured in ice cubes first and then combined with extremely cold water to create an ice lantern, the food color tends to stay put.

To help illustrate, I made the bucket see-through.

1 FOOD COLOR

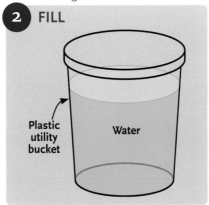

2 FILL

Plastic
utility
bucket

Water

STEP 1: Make about 8-10 standard trays of ice cubes with two drops of food color per cube. Add more food color if making larger cubes, less if smaller. Once frozen solid, release the cubes from the molds and store them in plastic bags in below-freezing temps until ready to use.

STEP 2: Fill one of the 5-gallon utility buckets with water until approximately 3/4 full. Put the bucket outdoors in below-freezing temps or in a deep freezer to chill.

If air temp is 0°F, chill for 6 hours. If colder, reduce the freezing time and if warmer, increase the freezing time.

The goal is to chill the water, not to freeze it. If ice begins to form, break it up and stir the water.

3 PLACE PIPE

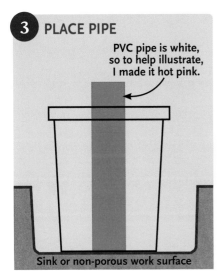

PVC pipe is white, so to help illustrate, I made it hot pink.

Sink or non-porous work surface

STEP 3: In a sink or on a non-porous work surface, position the PVC pipe in the center of the second 5-gallon bucket.

4 ADD CLEAR ICE CUBES

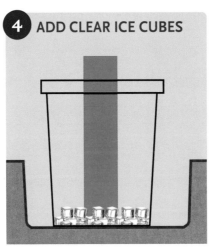

STEP 4: Pour approximately 2" of clear ice cubes around the PVC pipe to keep it centered and upright in the bucket.

5 COLORED ICE CUBES

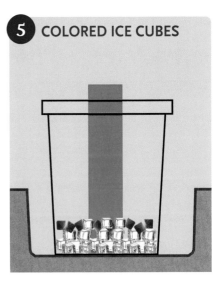

STEP 5: Sprinkle a handful of colored ice cubes on top of the clear ice cubes. Fill in with a few more clear cubes.

6 MORE LAYERS

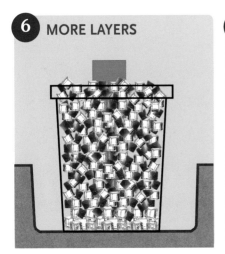

STEP 6: Randomly, or in a chosen pattern, layer in colored and clear ice cubes until the bucket is full. When using two or more colors, add clear ice cubes in between the colored cubes. Combining many colored ice cubes would be an interesting experiment!

7 INSULATE BOTTOM

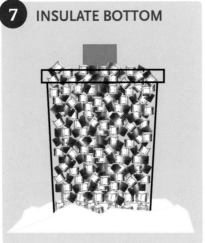

STEP 7: Place the bucket filled with ice cubes on snow or frozen ground in cold temps outdoors or on Styrofoam in a freezer. Make sure the bucket is level.

TIP

THREE COLORS?
When deciding which colors to use, keep in mind how food color blends:

Red+blue = purple
Blue+yellow = green
Yellow+red = orange
Red+blue+yellow = brown

8 · ADD WATER

STEP 8: Pour the chilled water from the first bucket into the PVC pipe so the water gently fills the ice cube bucket from the bottom up.

9 · TOP

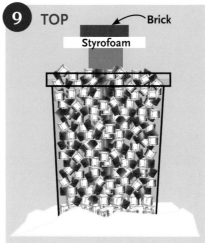

STEP 9: Top off the pipe with insulating material to keep the water inside the pipe from freezing. If outdoors, weigh down the foam with a rock or brick to keep it from blowing away.

10 · FREEZE

STEP 10: Let the container freeze for at least 12 hours at 0°F until the ice cubes and added water are frozen together. The water in the pipe must remain unfrozen.

You'll need more freezing time if temps are warmer, less if colder.

11 · EMPTY

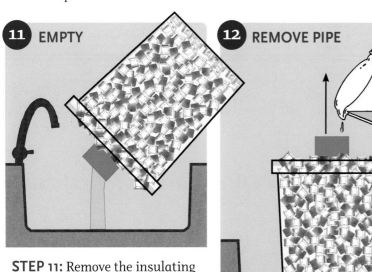

STEP 11: Remove the insulating top from the pipe and pour all unfrozen water from the bucket.

12 · REMOVE PIPE

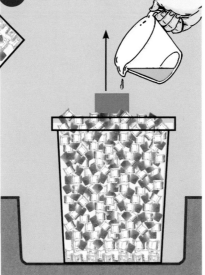

STEP 12: Pour warm water into the pipe until it loosens and can be pulled up and free of the ice.

13 · REMOVE BUCKET

STEP 13: Place the bucket upside down in a sink or bathtub to thaw for 15-30 minutes.

The bucket will release from the ice lantern and can be lifted off.

14 STORE

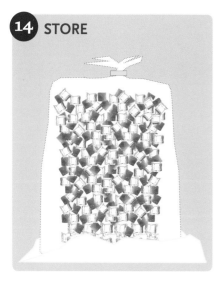

STEP 14: Place the lantern on or in a plastic bag in below-freezing temps (outdoors or in a freezer) until ready to use.

15 LIGHT IT UP

STEP 15: Both ends of the ice lantern should be open, so there's no need to drill a chimney. Place the ice lantern on a fire-resistant surface. Lower a candle in a candle holder into the ice lantern and light it. The light will bounce off the ice-cube edges and reflect the colors in the ice cubes, too!

15 ALT: LED LIGHTS

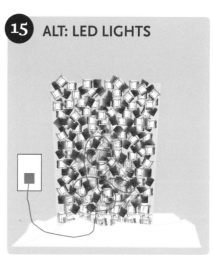

ALT STEP 15: Fill the cavity of the ice lantern with a string of LED lights intended for outdoor use. Place the ice lantern on the ground in the desired location and turn on the lights.

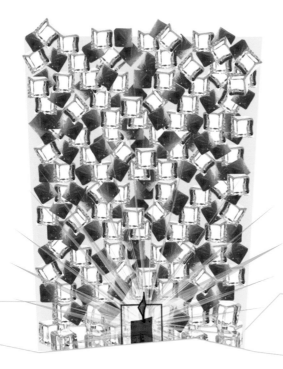

*The cut-glass appearance
of a Finnish lantern imitates
the unique dazzle of crystal. Although
slightly fussy to make, this lantern
is well worth the effort.*
**— Photo by Jennifer
Shea Hedberg**

Finnish Glass Ice Lantern

Originally named "clown ice lanterns" because of the balloons used to create the ice voids, these elegant ice lanterns needed a better name. When a friend likened them to glass vases she had seen in Finland, I changed the name in a split second. The balloons may be left in the ice if you like, but when removed they leave behind beautiful strings of air pockets that reflect the light.

To help illustrate, I made the bucket see-through.

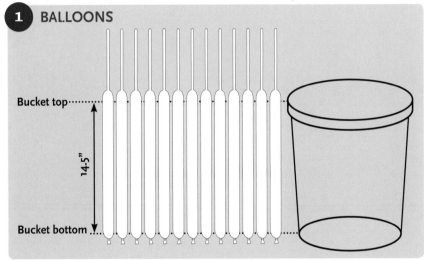

1 BALLOONS

Bucket top ⋯⋯

14.5"

Bucket bottom ⋯⋯

STEP 1: A 5-gallon utility bucket is 14.5" high. Inflate 12-14 twisting animal balloons with the air pump so they're a little longer than the bucket is high — about 17" long. ***Do not inflate all the way.***

2 TWISTING

STEP 2: Work with a single balloon at a time. Twist one balloon into random segments. Make the first twist and then hold that end between your knees while completing all twists. Even when done twisting, always hold both ends to keep the balloon from untwisting.

WHAT YOU NEED

Heavy-duty
5-gallon utility bucket

Utility bucket lid

12-14 twisting
animal balloons
(white or light blue
preferred)

Air pump
with balloon adapter

Hot glue gun
with hot glue sticks

Scissors

Cold tap water

Cold temps
or deep freezer

Candle with candle holder
and matches
or LED lights

— OPTIONAL —

Utility bucket lid

3 MEASURE

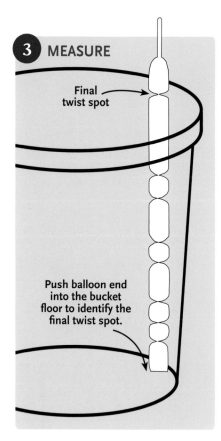

Final twist spot

Push balloon end into the bucket floor to identify the final twist spot.

STEP 3: Hold the twisted balloon up against the inside of the bucket with the tied end pushed into the bucket floor. With the forefinger and thumb of your other hand, pinch and make a final twist in the balloon just below the rim of the bucket. Continue to pinch and proceed to Step 4.

4 CUT AND TIE

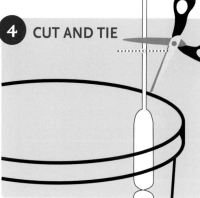

STEP 4: Hold the tied end of the balloon between your knees while pinching at the final twist spot. Snip off the uninflated tip of the balloon with a pair of scissors. Release the extra air above the pinch point.

Tie off the balloon at the last pinch point and cut off any extra balloon above the new knot.

5 HOT GLUE

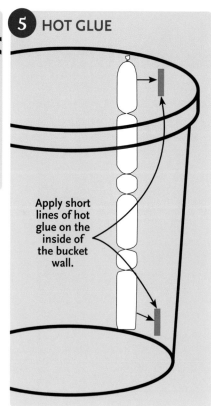

Apply short lines of hot glue on the inside of the bucket wall.

STEP 5: Apply 2 strips of hot glue to the inside of the bucket. The glue strips only need to be about 1" long. Count to 10 to let the glue cool down a bit. (The balloon may pop if the glue is too hot.) Press the bottom end of the twisted balloon into the floor of the bucket just in front of the bottom line of glue, then press the side of the balloon against the bottom strip of glue. Hold the bottom of the balloon in place while gently pulling the balloon taut and then press the top part of the balloon onto the top strip of glue. Hold the balloon in place for 10 seconds or until it's secure.

6 REPEAT

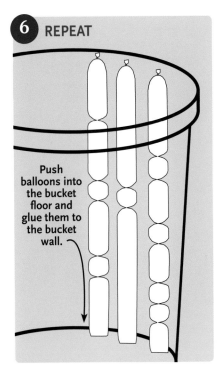

Push balloons into the bucket floor and glue them to the bucket wall.

STEP 6: Repeat with other balloons in a random pattern around the perimeter of the bucket. Some of the balloons could be added untwisted.

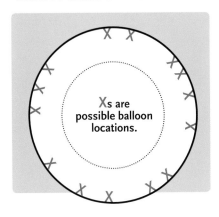

Xs are possible balloon locations.

7 ADD WATER

STEP 7: Put the prepared container where it will freeze. Make sure it's sitting on snow, frozen ground or insulation to keep the water at the bucket floor from freezing. Put the end of a garden hose into the bucket until it reaches the bottom. Turn on the water so that it flows *gently* into the bucket. (Garden hose not available? Bring water to the bucket, but pour gently!)

Why gently? The balloons are held in place with a small amount of hot glue. Too much glue and you won't be able to slide the ice out of the bucket. Too little glue and the balloons can become dislodged when adding water or moving the water-filled bucket.

8 FREEZE

STEP 8: Let the container freeze for about 6-12 hours and then put a lid on it. The lid will provide insulation to keep the top ice thin. Lift the lid to check the thickness of the ice.

Ideally, the perimeter of the ice should be about 3" thick. Depending on the temperature, the freezing process could take anywhere from 12 to 48 hours. At 0°F, check after 24 hours. Continue to freeze if more time is needed, checking every 6 hours. (*TIP:* The slower the water freezes, the clearer the ice.)

9 THAW AND TWIST

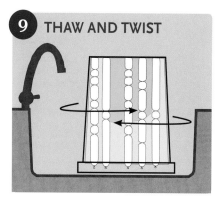

10 POUR

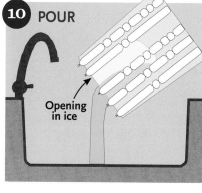

Opening
in ice

11 REMOVE BALLOONS

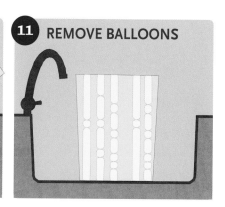

STEP 9: When the ice is done freezing, put the bucket upside down in a sink and let it thaw for 15-30 minutes.

Hot glue anchors the ice to the inside of the bucket, so a Finnish ice lantern will not slide out as easily as a bucket ice lantern.

If after 30 minutes the lantern doesn't slide out of the bucket, remove any exposed hot glue. Then turn the bucket upside down and twist sharply from side to side. Repeat the twisting motions until the ice slides into the sink.

STEP 10: The upside-down ice lantern should be filled with water with a hole in the top of the ice. (If the hole has frozen over, the ice can be chipped open using a knife or screwdriver.) Pour the remaining water from the lantern into the sink.

STEP 11: Pop each balloon and, with your fingers or a pair of tweezers, gently remove it from the ice. You might have to chisel into the ice to remove remaining balloon bits.

12 STORE

13 LIGHT

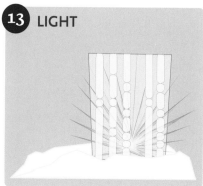

STEP 12: Place the lantern in a plastic bag in below-freezing temps (outdoors or in the freezer) until ready to display.

STEP 13: When ready to use the lantern, either stuff the cavity with LED lights or drill a chimney and put it over a bright candle.

TIP

FUN IDEA
Having trouble removing the balloons? Use brightly colored twisting animal balloons instead. Leave the balloons in the ice for a festive Mardi Gras effect!

The tiers of this Finnish glass ice
lantern tower are shaped in
garbage can-sized buckets
and fused together.
The tower is lit by suspending candles
through a central hole, which extends
from top to bottom.
— Photo by Stephen L. Garrett

The multi-faceted quality of an ice chip tower creates a wonderful focal point in a large ice luminary landscape.
— Photo by Jennifer Shea Hedberg

BUILDING SAFELY

FREEZE TOGETHER
An ice construction can slip apart if its pieces haven't fully frozen together. Only build with ice in below-freezing temps.

LEVEL ICE
Flat wet ice surfaces may meld together in below-freezing temps, but an ice structure will be safer if each of the ice pieces has been leveled as well.

GLUE WISELY
It's tempting to use snice (a mixture of snow and water) to "glue" ice together, but when it gets warm snice melts faster than ice. The gaps created can make your ice structure unsafe. Use flat, level, wet ice surfaces for the strongest ice bonds.

ONLY ICE
It's also tempting to use wood or metal with the ice to try to make it stronger. Unfortunately, when it starts to melt it will quickly become unsafe. *Why?* When ice melts, it sticks to itself. When ice melts off metal or wood, it falls off.

BIGGER IS DANGEROUS!
I love to make big ice structures because they're visually stunning. But large pieces of ice are extremely heavy and, if they fall, can seriously injure someone.

Please pay attention to these warnings and stay safe!

Building with Ice

Stacking ice on ice and lighting it up is an exciting challenge. We've discussed "gluing" ice together *(see p 80)*, but it's worth repeating that two wet, flat surfaces placed together create a tight seal in cold temps. Candles inside ice lanterns need air to burn brightly and melting ice needs an escape.

A FEW THINGS TO CONSIDER:

Chimney Creation
Drilling a chimney provides a way for heated air to escape. Drilling a hole to allow air in to feed a candle is also essential. Both steps are important when building tall ice structures like an *Ice Person Lantern (see p 165)*.

Using Snow
Snow is indispensable when working with ice glass and building ice structures. It's used to hold ice glass in place — like the many ice petals used to make an *Ice Flower (see p 169)*. Snow is also helpful when trying to level an ice structure or facilitate air flow.

Water Management
When an ice lantern is glued and sealed to any hard surface or a piece of ice glass, as in an *Ice Glass Sculpture (see p 175)*, consider how the melting ice will escape. A strategically placed hole drilled into the ice lantern will enable water to flow out.

Beautiful Imperfection
I built my first *Ice Chip Tower (see p 183)* after a sheet of ice glass shattered during transport. Left with hundreds of small ice glass pieces, I created a luminary ice structure that has become a mainstay in my installations. When the imperfection of ice is embraced, new opportunities arise.

Success Requires Finishing
The plans and techniques revealed in a *Basic Ice Bar (see p 191)* expand upon the finishing and leveling skills necessary to build larger structures with ice.

Planning with Molds
When designing an elaborate ice luminary creation with molded ice like the *Miniature Ice Castle (see p 199)*, the size of the entire structure is determined by the mold shape with limited sizing options.

Experiment
Use your imagination and come up with more ideas!

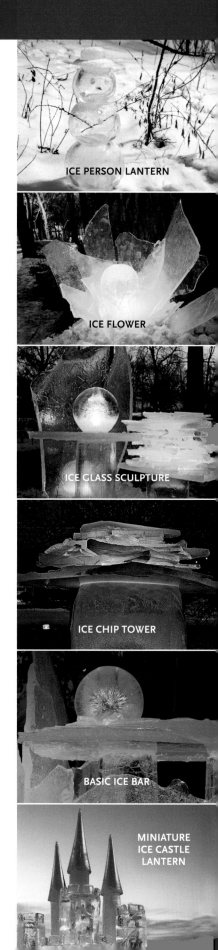

ICE PERSON LANTERN

ICE FLOWER

ICE GLASS SCULPTURE

ICE CHIP TOWER

BASIC ICE BAR

MINIATURE ICE CASTLE LANTERN

This ice person was created by Mary Arneson. She let the sun light it up, but ice people can be lit with LED lights or candles, too.
— Photo by Stephen L. Garrett

Ice Person Lantern

Globe ice lanterns made with heavyweight balloons are meant to be round, but their shape can make them challenging to stack. Adding a puff of air into the balloons before clipping and freezing them will flatten the lantern tops so they'll stack easily. You can make a playful ice person to dress up with an ice hat, some ice buttons, a few twigs and even a baby carrot for a nose. This guy, pictured left, was not lit when this photo was taken, but it's easy to do with a little planning.

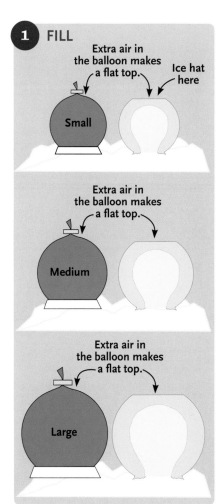

1 FILL

Extra air in the balloon makes a flat top.

Ice hat here

Small

Extra air in the balloon makes a flat top.

Medium

Extra air in the balloon makes a flat top.

Large

STEP 1: Make 3 globe ice lanterns (1 small, 1 medium, 1 large). Follow directions on page 29 with one exception — make flat tops.

To make flat tops: Blow a little extra air into the balloon before clipping it closed. ***Why?*** The air will rise to the top inside the balloon, forming a flat top when the water freezes.

Continue following the directions on page 30 to finish making the lanterns.

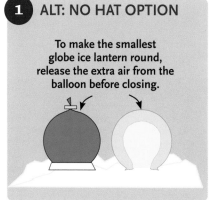

1 ALT: NO HAT OPTION

To make the smallest globe ice lantern round, release the extra air from the balloon before closing.

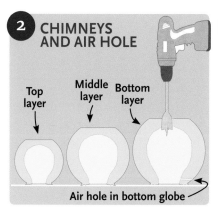

② CHIMNEYS AND AIR HOLE

Top layer
Middle layer
Bottom layer

Air hole in bottom globe

STEP 2: Position the globe ice lanterns with the large openings facing down. Drill wide (1"-1.5") chimney holes in the tops of each globe and a small air hole in the side near the bottom of the largest globe.

Molded ice in many different shapes and sizes can be stacked and lit using the same flatten-wet-stack method.
— Photo by Stephen L. Garrett

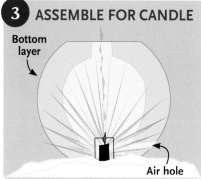

③ ASSEMBLE FOR CANDLE

Bottom layer

Air hole

STEP 3: Place the candle on the ground and light. Put the largest globe over the candle and stabilize it. Check air flow to candle.

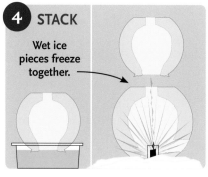

④ STACK

Wet ice pieces freeze together.

STEP 4: Wet the underside of the middle globe and position it over the chimney of the large bottom globe. Check air flow.

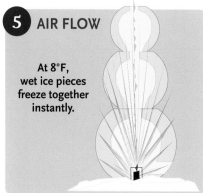

⑤ AIR FLOW

At 8°F, wet ice pieces freeze together instantly.

STEP 5: Wet and stack the final globe. Check air flow.

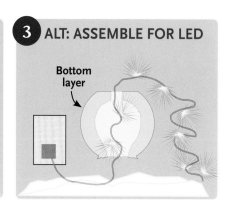

③ ALT: ASSEMBLE FOR LED

Bottom layer

ALT STEP 3: Put the plug end of a string of lights through the top chimney and out the bottom of the largest globe ice lantern. Plug in the lights and position the globe. Use snow to level it.

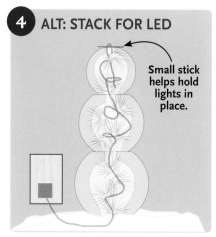

④ ALT: STACK FOR LED

Small stick helps hold lights in place.

ALT STEP 4: Wet the bottom of each globe and lace the lights through the bottom and out the top of each globe before setting in place. Repeat. The lights can be secured to the top globe by looping the end of the string of lights over a small stick and then tucking it back inside the top globe.

6 ADD ICE HAT

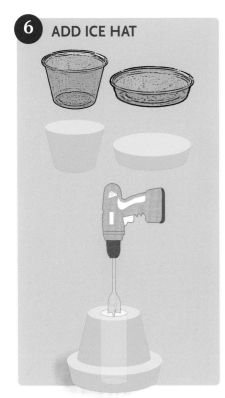

STEP 6: Fill the small plastic containers with water and allow them to freeze solid. Thaw briefly and remove ice from plastic. Flatten the contact surfaces and glue the two larger ice pieces together *(see p 80).*

Using a candle? A chimney must be drilled all the way through the assembled hat before it's placed over the ice person's top hole.

FINISHING TOUCHES

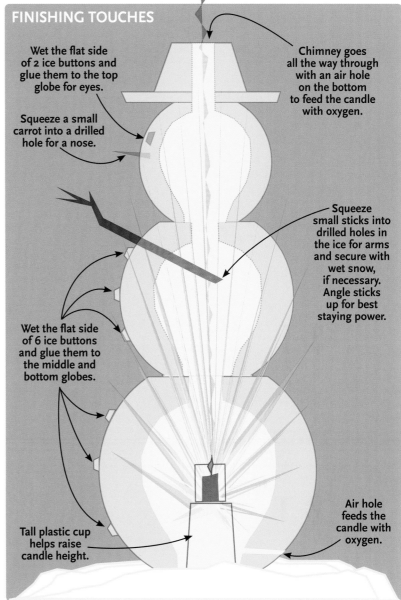

Wet the flat side of 2 ice buttons and glue them to the top globe for eyes.

Squeeze a small carrot into a drilled hole for a nose.

Chimney goes all the way through with an air hole on the bottom to feed the candle with oxygen.

Squeeze small sticks into drilled holes in the ice for arms and secure with wet snow, if necessary. Angle sticks up for best staying power.

Wet the flat side of 6 ice buttons and glue them to the middle and bottom globes.

Tall plastic cup helps raise candle height.

Air hole feeds the candle with oxygen.

7 ADD ICE BUTTONS

Colored crepe paper or Food color

STEP 7: Ice buttons can be used for eyes, too. Fill 8 tiny plastic containers (such as salad dressing cups) with water. To add color, try a few drops of food color. For a less messy option, add small strips of colored crepe paper to the water. Allow the water in the cups to freeze solid, then thaw briefly and remove the ice. Flatten the contact surfaces and glue them to the ice globes where desired. Your ice person has come alive!

 Ice Flower

An ice flower is created with a central ice lantern of any shape surrounded by pieces of ice glass. For this project, I use a teardrop ice lantern inserted point-side down in a large pile of snow to serve as the flower's center. The smallest pieces of ice glass encircle the teardrop lantern and larger pieces of ice glass spiral out simulating flower petals. I love to build ice flowers up against a tree as it seems like a natural place to find them. Ice flowers also are charming nestled in a large pot of snow and greens by the front door.

1 TEARDROP ICE LANTERN

STEP 1: Make a teardrop ice lantern according to directions on page 83.

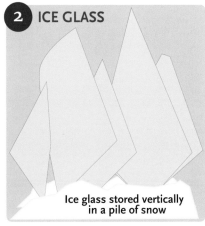

2 ICE GLASS

Ice glass stored vertically in a pile of snow

STEP 2: Create about a dozen pieces of ice glass according to directions on page 45.

Left: Every year during the Middlemoon Creekwalk, I build an ice flower next to an ancient cottonwood tree along the path. Not only is the tree magnificent in stature, but the shadow it casts amid the street lights creates a perfect dark spot to make the ice glass really glow.
— Photo by Jennifer Shea Hedberg

TIP

LEAVE A LIGHTING GAP
As you add ice petals around the central ice lantern, be sure to leave a gap so you can reach in to light or replace the candle.

WHAT YOU NEED

Snow

Teardrop ice lantern

Ice glass

Paint scraper

Floating candle

Matches

— OPTIONAL —

Torch

3 LOCATION

Snow pile

STEP 3: Choose a location for the ice flower and create a foundation by placing several shovelfuls of snow into a pile.

4 DRILL

Drill a small drainage hole.

STEP 4: Drill a small hole in the teardrop lantern for drainage. While this isn't essential, it will help the candle burn brightly for longer.

5 POINT DOWN

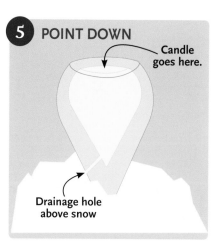

Candle goes here.

Drainage hole above snow

STEP 5: Place the teardrop ice lantern into the snow pile with the pointed end down, leaving the drilled hole above the snow.

6 CHECK

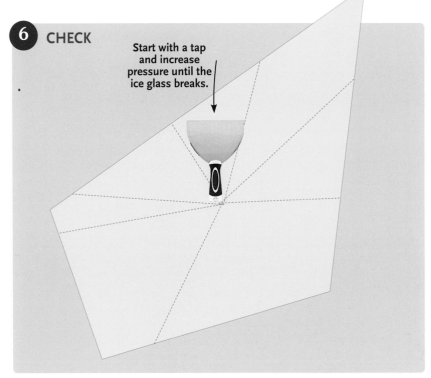

Start with a tap and increase pressure until the ice glass breaks.

7 FIRST RING

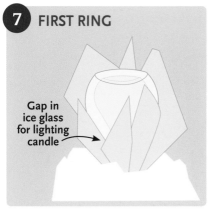

Gap in ice glass for lighting candle

STEP 7: Encircle the teardrop lantern with small pieces of ice glass. Remember to keep the drainage hole clear of snow. Picture how flower petals over-lap each other and mimic that look with the ice glass pieces.

STEP 6: *If you have small pieces of ice glass, disregard this step.* Lay a large piece of ice glass flat on the snow. With the handle of a paint scraper, sharply tap the center of the ice until it breaks into random pieces. There is no guarantee about how the ice glass will break, so keep your mind and heart open to the infinite possibilities. Snow stops light, so scrape away any snow that sticks to the ice.

Ice flowers can be made in many sizes. Consider an ice flower cluster (left) or a tiny ice flower with a votive candle holder as the center (below).

This young gentleman (left) was thrilled to take home an ice shard of his own after watching the building of an ice flower. — Photos by Jennifer Shea Hedberg

8 ADDITIONAL RINGS

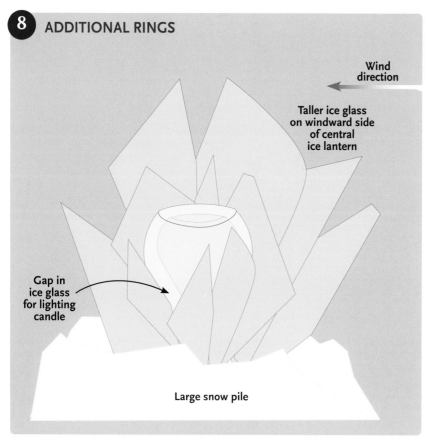

Wind direction

Taller ice glass on windward side of central ice lantern

Gap in ice glass for lighting candle

Large snow pile

9 LIGHT IT UP!

STEP 9: Put a floating candle in the cavity of the teardrop ice lantern just in case the drainage hole plugs up and the cavity fills with water. Light and enjoy!

STEP 8: Add more ice glass around the first ring, using progressively larger pieces of ice glass as you go. Make sure that you leave a gap in the ice glass so you can reach in to place the candle and light it. Don't position the gap in a place that could leave your candle vulnerable to the wind.

This unique ice flower was created with bubble ice glass
I discovered while working at an ice castle in Lincoln, New Hampshire.
This kind of ice glass is created when a fine mist of water is sprayed over snow
in below-freezing temps. It snows often in the White Mountains and the master
builders of Ice Castles spray water constantly to build up their glacial palace.
Bubble ice was everywhere. I just had to pull it free, scrape off snow and torch away
the haze. I had plenty of wavy ice glass to surround a large teardrop lantern.
— Photo by Patrick Groleau

✳✳ Ice Glass
✳✳ Sculpture

Ice glass is most beautiful when combined with ice lanterns to create a visual symphony of candlelight. When you're wanting color and convenience, use colored LED lights for an easy theatrical presentation.

When I made the sculpture at left I had one extraordinary globe ice lantern, so I decided to make it the focal point. Putting it on an ice pedestal and adding a candle did the trick. I surrounded it with majestic shards of ice glass and lit them from behind with a few more globe ice lanterns at ground level.

1 MAKE ICE PIECES

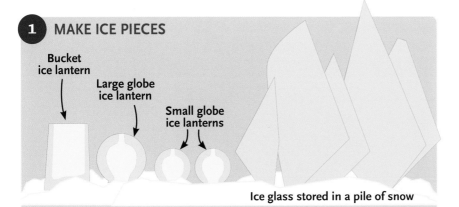

Bucket ice lantern

Large globe ice lantern

Small globe ice lanterns

Ice glass stored in a pile of snow

STEP 1: Make several pieces of ice glass, a bucket ice lantern, a large globe ice lantern and several smaller globe ice lanterns. Store them all at below-freezing temps until ready to use.

Left: Key strategies for assembling ice glass sculptures include leveling the structure and torching the snow haze from the ice. Doing these two things will greatly improve the appearance of your creations.

Right: Amazing color can be added to ice with projectable LED lights.
— Photos by Jennifer Shea Hedberg

TIP
KEEP IN MIND
Ice glass is organically shaped, so each ice glass sculpture will be unique. The final look of your sculpture will depend on the ice lanterns and ice glass you have on hand.

WHAT YOU NEED

Ice glass

Bucket ice lantern

Large globe ice lantern
with drilled chimney

Smaller globe ice lanterns
with drilled chimneys

Large leveling tool

Small plastic cup

Power drill
with 3/8" and 1"
spade bits

Paint scraper

Torch

Candle
and candle holder

Fireplace Matches

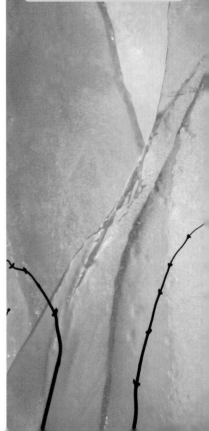

2 CREATE THE BASE

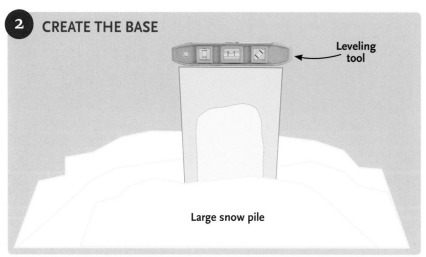

Leveling tool

Large snow pile

STEP 2: Place a bucket ice lantern in the middle of a large pile of snow. The lantern is the base of the sculpture so it must be level. Place a leveling tool on the lantern's top and push snow or small ice pieces underneath the lantern until it's level.

3 SELECT ICE

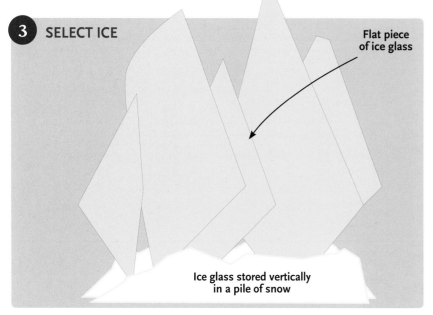

Flat piece of ice glass

Ice glass stored vertically in a pile of snow

STEP 3: Choose a flat piece of ice glass from your collection. Make sure it's slightly larger than the top of the bucket ice lantern or break off a piece from a much larger sheet.

4 LOOSEN ICE

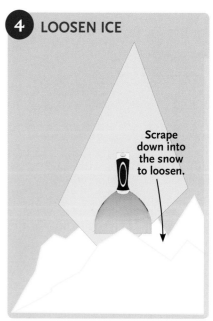

Scrape down into the snow to loosen.

STEP 4: To loosen a piece of ice glass stored in a pile of snow, hold it with one hand while using a paint scraper to scrape into the snow with the other hand. Scrape down both sides of the ice glass to separate it from the snow. *Do not push against the ice glass,* but rock it from side to side until it's loose and can be pulled free.

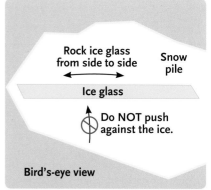

Rock ice glass from side to side

Snow pile

Ice glass

Do NOT push against the ice.

Bird's-eye view

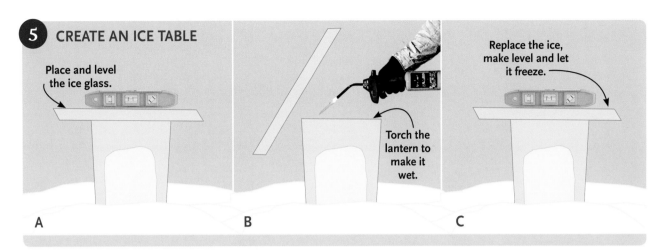

5 CREATE AN ICE TABLE

Place and level the ice glass.

Torch the lantern to make it wet.

Replace the ice, make level and let it freeze.

A

B

C

STEP 5: (A) Place the ice glass on top of the bucket ice lantern and turn it until it's level. **(B)**Remove the ice glass and torch the top of the bucket lantern to make it wet. **(C)**Replace the ice glass on the wet lantern top and use ice and/or snow to make it level. Wait until the two ice pieces are frozen together to add more ice.

6 DRILL AIR HOLE

Hole on side near bottom

STEP 6: Drill a small hole using a 3/8" spade bit in the side of the large globe ice lantern as close to the bottom as possible. *Why?* The ice globe will freeze tightly to the ice table, so it needs a way for air to get in to feed the candle and for melting ice to escape.

7 PLACE CANDLE AND GLOBE ICE LANTERN

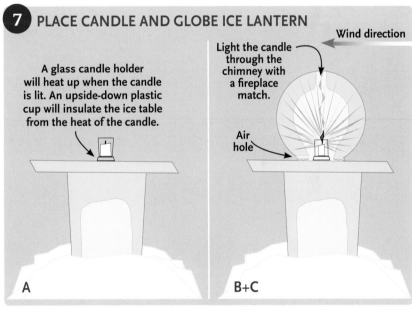

A glass candle holder will heat up when the candle is lit. An upside-down plastic cup will insulate the ice table from the heat of the candle.

Wind direction

Light the candle through the chimney with a fireplace match.

Air hole

A

B+C

STEP 7: (A) Place the plastic cup and candle in a candle holder on the ice table, centering it above the bucket ice lantern. **(B)**Place the large globe lantern over the candle with its large opening facing down and the side air hole positioned away from the wind. Look down the lantern chimney to make sure it's positioned directly above the candle. **(C)**Light the candle through the chimney with a fireplace match. The slight ice melt from the candle's heat will secure the ice lantern to the ice table.

8 SELECT ICE GLASS

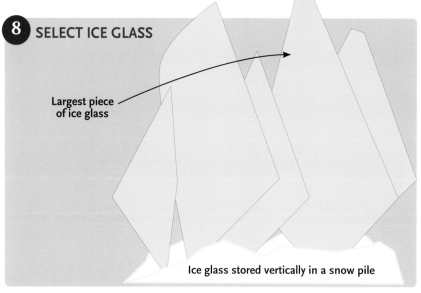

Largest piece
of ice glass

Ice glass stored vertically in a snow pile

STEP 8: Select the largest piece of ice glass.

9 PLACE ICE GLASS

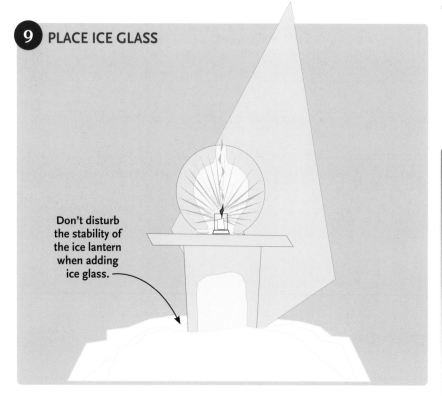

Don't disturb
the stability of
the ice lantern
when adding
ice glass.

STEP 9: Insert one end of the largest ice glass piece into the snow behind the lit globe ice lantern. Try not to disturb the stability or the air flow of the lantern. Add extra snow or snice near the base of the ice glass and hold it until the ice feels stable.

10 REPEAT

STEP 10: Place more ice glass pieces at various angles, adding extra snow or snice near the bases of the ice glass to secure.

TIP

SECURING ICE GLASS
In warmer temps (15°F to 32°F), it's easy to pack snow around the base of ice glass to secure it. But snow freezes to ice slowly at these temps, so ice glass will be most secure if inserted vertically. In colder temps (below 15°F), ice glass will freeze quickly into snow — so with a little snice (see p 43), it can be positioned at more extreme angles.

11 | ADD MORE LIGHT

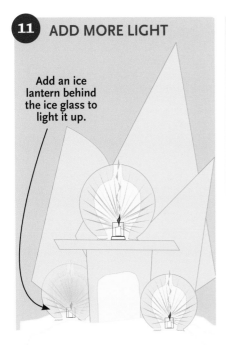

Add an ice lantern behind the ice glass to light it up.

STEP 11: Set up one or more small globe ice lanterns behind the ice glass shards in the snow. This will light up the ice from behind. Add another small globe ice lantern in front to add more visual interest.

A SCULPTURE IN 3-D

This photo shows a different perspective of the sculpture on page 174. Notice how the smaller globe ice lantern placed in the back can now be seen tucked between the angled shards of ice glass. From this side, the ice table topped with the large globe ice lantern can be seen through the large sheet of ice glass.

The photo also shows a short ice chip tower *(see p 183)* added to one side. Consider adding more ice lanterns and ice glass, keeping in mind that the trick is knowing when to stop. Continue to experiment with ice placement to discover how light bounces off the angles and edges.

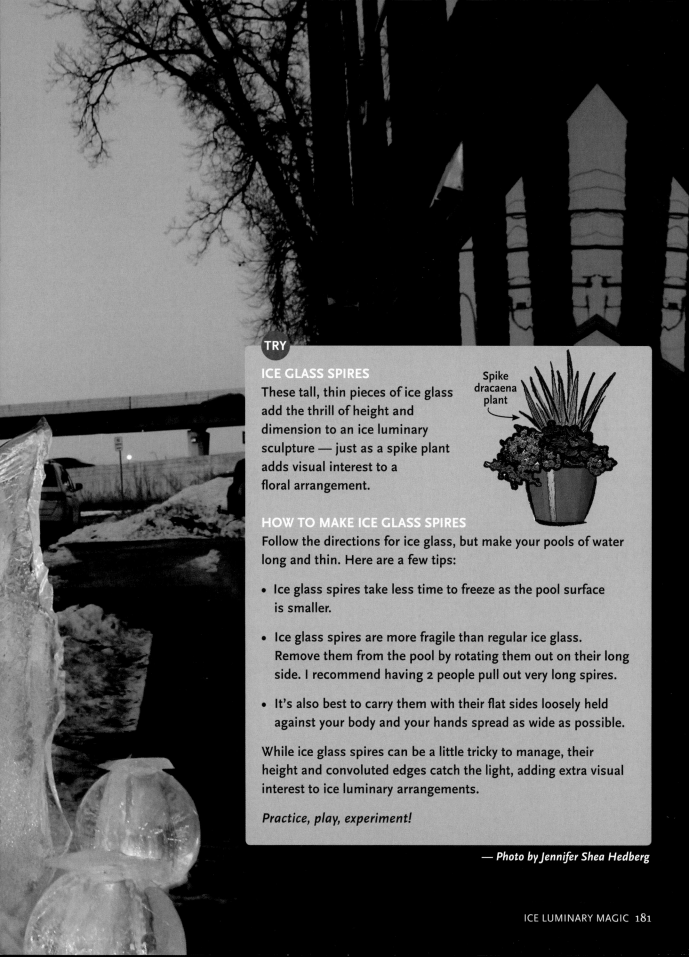

TRY

ICE GLASS SPIRES

These tall, thin pieces of ice glass add the thrill of height and dimension to an ice luminary sculpture — just as a spike plant adds visual interest to a floral arrangement.

Spike dracaena plant

HOW TO MAKE ICE GLASS SPIRES

Follow the directions for ice glass, but make your pools of water long and thin. Here are a few tips:

- Ice glass spires take less time to freeze as the pool surface is smaller.

- Ice glass spires are more fragile than regular ice glass. Remove them from the pool by rotating them out on their long side. I recommend having 2 people pull out very long spires.

- It's also best to carry them with their flat sides loosely held against your body and your hands spread as wide as possible.

While ice glass spires can be a little tricky to manage, their height and convoluted edges catch the light, adding extra visual interest to ice luminary arrangements.

Practice, play, experiment!

— *Photo by Jennifer Shea Hedberg*

Ice Chip Tower

A sheet of ice glass can break unexpectedly during harvesting, but like many things about ice and life, accidents can create new opportunities and great beauty. A case in point is the first ice chip tower I made while building the Enchanted Forest for the 2010 City of Lakes Luminary Loppet. With the shimmering towers of the Icecropolis looming just around the bend, I wanted to go vertical whenever possible. I assembled dozens of large ice glass sheets and garbage can-sized ice pedestals to create a forest of ice. Several sheets of ice glass broke during transport, so I opted to improvise. With one ice pedestal remaining and nothing to put on it, I used all I had left — small ice glass pieces, which I now call ice chips.

WHAT YOU NEED

Ice glass pieces

Bucket ice lantern with level top

Power drill with 3/8" and 1" spade bits

4" x 24" PVC pipe

5-gallon utility bucket

Torch

Paint scraper

Plastic cup

Floating candle and matches

1 **ICE GLASS**

Store vertically in snow

2 **BUCKET ICE LANTERN**

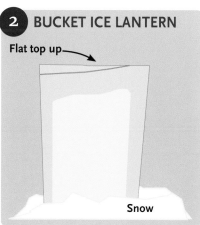

Flat top up

Snow

STEP 1: Make several pieces of ice glass *(see p 45)*. Reserve one or two large pieces and break the rest into small pieces or use remnant pieces from another ice glass project. ***TIP:*** It's much easier to build an ice chip tower when all pieces are the same thickness.

STEP 2: Make a partial-freeze bucket ice lantern using a 5-gallon bucket *(see p 19)*. ***Ice top not level?*** About 6 hours before your ice lantern is ready, add a small amount of water to the top of the ice. Once the new water layer is frozen, release the ice lantern from the bucket and pour out the remaining water.

Left: This ice chip tower is really a garbage can-sized pedestal with an ice glass tabletop and an ice chip tower on top. It welcomed visitors to the Luminary Loppet's Enchanted Forest in Minneapolis.
— Photo by Rob Nopola

3 DRILL AIR HOLE

STEP 3: If you plan to illuminate the bucket ice lantern with a candle, drill a small hole into the side of the lantern toward the top of the hollow chamber. This hole will allow the heat of the candle to escape.

If you want to use LED lights, disregard Steps 3-5.

4 CREATE MOUSEHOLE

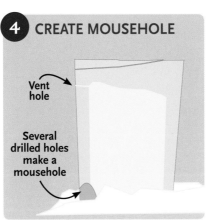

STEP 4: Create a mousehole at the base of the ice lantern so you can light or replace the candle after you've built the ice chip tower.

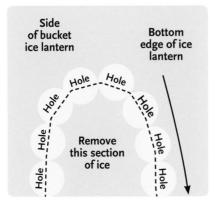

Using a 1" spade bit, gently drill an arc-shaped series of holes into the side of the bucket ice lantern near the bottom. Remove the center portion of ice. The hole should be large enough for your hand to pass through. The points of ice in the mousehole can be chipped off with a chisel and smoothed with a torch.

5 LEVEL

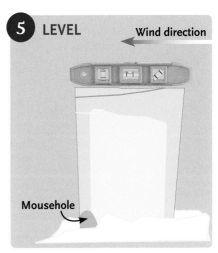

STEP 5: Position the ice lantern on the surface where you'll display your ice chip tower with the mousehole facing away from the wind. Use a leveling tool to ensure that the lantern top is level. Use snow and small bits of ice glass to prop up and secure the lantern in place.

If you place the ice lantern in snow, be sure that the mousehole is accessible and that your hand can pass into the lantern. Before the snow hardens, create a level spot inside the lantern for the candle. Once you've built your ice chip tower, you won't be able to make adjustments.

To help illustrate, I made the white PVC pipe hot pink.

6 ICE GLASS TABLETOP

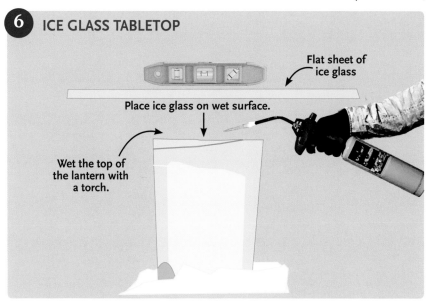

Flat sheet of ice glass

Place ice glass on wet surface.

Wet the top of the lantern with a torch.

7 PVC PIPE

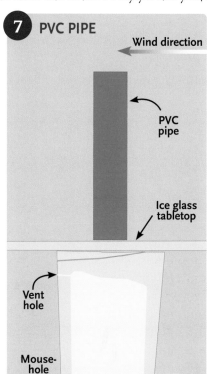

Wind direction

PVC pipe

Ice glass tabletop

Vent hole

Mouse-hole

STEP 6: Use a paint scraper to remove all snow from a large piece of ice glass and place it on the top of the bucket ice lantern so that it balances nicely. Rotate it until it fits and looks the way you'd like. Use a leveling tool to see if you need to add ice chips, snow or snice to level it.

Remove the ice glass and use a torch to wet the entire top of the ice lantern. Reposition the ice glass and allow the two ice surfaces to freeze together. (Ice will fuse immediately at 8°F.)

Snow will stop the light, so only add snow or snice in between ice pieces if necessary to level or fuse them. If the pieces don't freeze together, wait for colder temps to continue building.

STEP 7: Place the PVC pipe on the ice glass directly above the center of the bucket ice lantern.

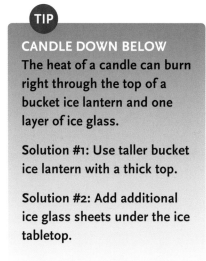

TIP

CANDLE DOWN BELOW
The heat of a candle can burn right through the top of a bucket ice lantern and one layer of ice glass.

Solution #1: Use taller bucket ice lantern with a thick top.

Solution #2: Add additional ice glass sheets under the ice tabletop.

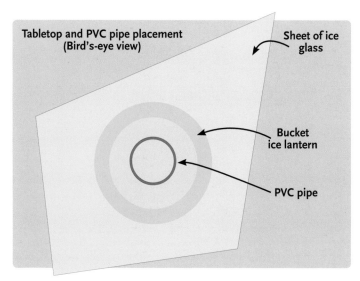

Tabletop and PVC pipe placement (Bird's-eye view)

Sheet of ice glass

Bucket ice lantern

PVC pipe

8 BREAK UP

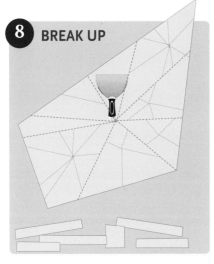

STEP 8: Collect remnant ice glass pieces or break up a large sheet of ice glass into smaller pieces.

To break up ice glass: Lay a sheet of ice glass flat with a booted toe under one edge. Using the handle of a paint scraper, forcefully tap the ice glass in the center. It should break into several pieces. Continue to break up the ice until you have a dozen or so pieces to start building.

TIP: Break up "uninteresting" pieces of ice glass first. I consider large square pieces uninteresting, but use your own eye.

9 FIRST ICE GLASS LAYER

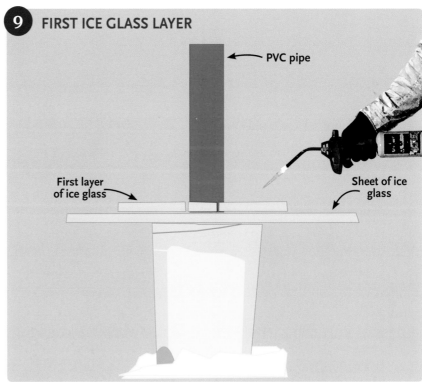

STEP 9: Choose an ice glass chip and remove excess snow with a paint scraper. Lay it next to the PVC pipe. Repeat with more pieces of ice glass, placing them around the PVC pipe to create the first tower layer. Lift one chip up and torch the ice glass underneath until it's wet. Replace the ice glass chip. Repeat this process with the other ice glass chips and allow the layer to freeze to the underlying sheet of ice glass before starting the next layer.

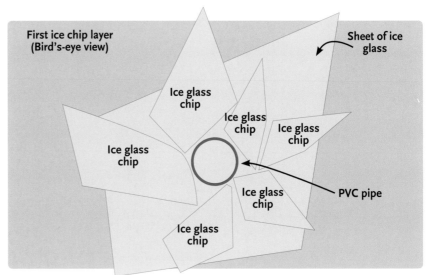

10 TWIST PVC

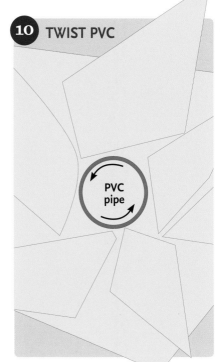

STEP 10: After adding each level of ice glass and allowing it to freeze, rotate the PVC slightly to keep it from freezing to the surface of the ice glass sheet.

11 ADD MORE LAYERS

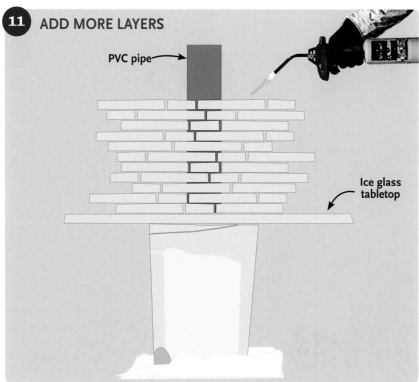

PVC pipe

Ice glass tabletop

STEP 11: Add additional layers of ice glass chips. Make sure each layer has a chance to freeze to the layer beneath it before proceeding with the next layer. *Remember to rotate the PVC pipe after each layer.*

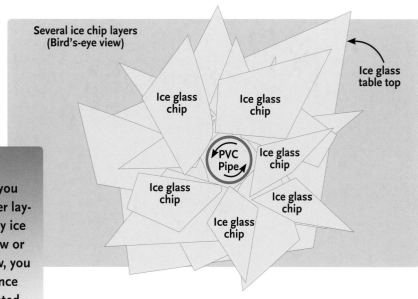

Several ice chip layers
(Bird's-eye view)

Ice glass table top

Ice glass chip

Ice glass chip

PVC Pipe

Ice glass chip

Ice glass chip

Ice glass chip

Ice glass chip

TIP

LEVELING LAYERS

Snow stops light. As you work to keep the tower layers level, try using tiny ice chips rather than snow or snice. If you use snow, you may see dark spots once your tower is illuminated.

12 REMOVE PVC PIPE

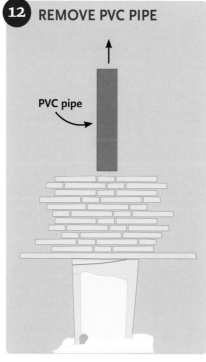

PVC pipe

STEP 12: After the last layer of ice chips has been created and has frozen into place, twist and gently lift the PVC pipe straight up and out of the ice chip tower.

13 LIGHT

Wind direction

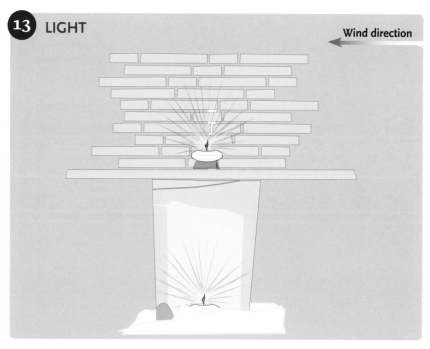

STEP 13: Place a votive candle, a floating candle or battery-operated LED lights in the empty space in the tower center and in the lower ice lantern to light up the whole thing.

TIP

KEEP THE CANDLE WHERE IT BELONGS
When putting a candle in the snow or on ice, remember to put an upside-down clear plastic cup underneath to both raise the candle's height and keep the candle from melting the ice surface.

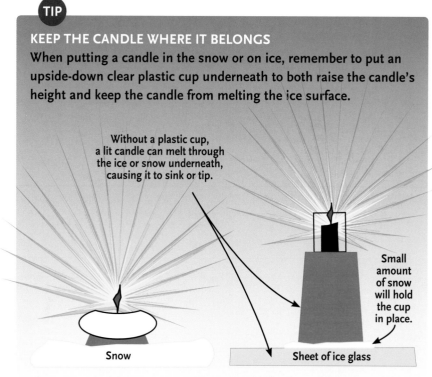

Without a plastic cup, a lit candle can melt through the ice or snow underneath, causing it to sink or tip.

Small amount of snow will hold the cup in place.

Snow

Sheet of ice glass

To help illustrate, I made the clear plastic cup hot pink.

TIP

CANDLE GOING OUT?
There could be gaps in the ice chip tower where wind can pass through and blow out your candle.

Solution #1: Put the candle in a tall clear candle holder.

Solution #2: Fill ice gaps on the windward side with small ice chips, snow or snice.

An ice chip tower and multiple ice luminary sculptures light up the front yard of one of my favorite clients. Thanks Mary and Dan for letting me play in your yard every year!
— Photo by Jennifer Shea Hedberg

This ice bar adorned with a leaf bucket ice lantern
serves as a magnet gathering people together
as they venture into the winter night.
— Photo by Per Breiehagen

✳✳ ✳✳ Basic Ice Bar
Made with Ice Glass

This is an exhilarating project, and its most important step involves carefully finishing and leveling the bucket ice lanterns used to create the ice bar's base. It's critical that three of the lanterns — the ones intended for the top row — are all the same height since they'll be sitting on ice and won't have the benefit of snow to help level them out. Size everything up before you head to the building site. Mark all your pieces so you'll remember which one goes where, then start creating your ice masterpiece.

Because this kind of ice bar is built with organically shaped ice glass, each creation is certain to have its own unique character. Surveying your ice glass collection and deciding how the pieces will fit together is a joyful part of the building process.

A. Make Ice Glass and Bucket Ice Lanterns

Create all your building components before you begin assembly. It's always a good idea to make a bit more than you think you'll need.

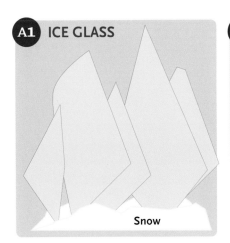

A1 ICE GLASS

Snow

A2 BUCKET ICE LANTERNS

Snow

STEP A1: Make pieces of ice glass *(see p 45)* at least 2" thick. Select two pieces for the bar tops. Make more ice glass — thinner and smaller — to use for decorations.

STEP A2: Make 6 bucket ice lanterns using 7-gallon utility buckets and the partial-freeze method *(see p 19)*.

B. Finishing and Leveling

It's essential to make the bucket ice lanterns as close to the same height as possible and to make sure that their tops are level. This will make fusing them together easier and help ensure that the ice bar stands straight.

Stand all lanterns on their flat bottoms (the surfaces that touched the bucket floors during freezing) and proceed to flatten the uneven tops.

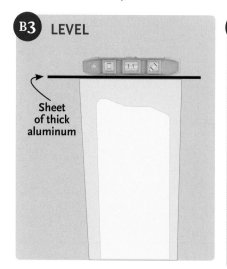

B1 CHISEL

STEP B1: If the tops of the ice lanterns are very uneven, use a chisel to remove the high points of the ice top.

B2 IRON FLAT

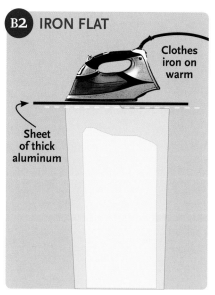

STEP B2: Continue to flatten the tops with a sheet of aluminum and a clothes iron.

B3 LEVEL

B4 ADJUST HEIGHT

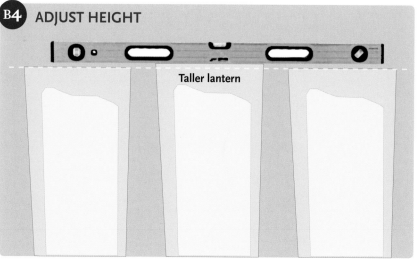

STEP B3: Place a leveling tool on the aluminum sheet to check if the top of each lantern is level. If not, use the iron with the aluminum sheet to remove more ice from the high side. Recheck with the level.

STEP B4: Separate the bucket ice lanterns into 2 groups of 3. The lanterns within each group should be very close in height. In the group shown above, the center ice lantern is too tall so ice must be removed from its top. Use the aluminum sheet and clothes iron to melt the extra ice, periodically checking to determine if all lanterns are of equal height.

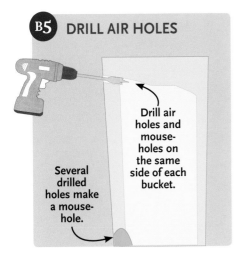

B5 DRILL AIR HOLES

Drill air holes and mouse-holes on the same side of each bucket.

Several drilled holes make a mouse-hole.

STEP B5: If you plan to light up your bar with candles, drill air holes into the sides of all the bucket lanterns so that hot air can escape. Use a 1/4" spade bit.

You'll also need to create mouse-holes near the bottom of the lanterns so that candles can be positioned, lit and relit. (For more on mouseholes, *see p 184.*)

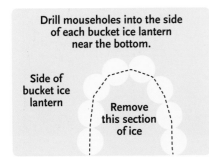

Drill mouseholes into the side of each bucket ice lantern near the bottom.

Side of bucket ice lantern

Remove this section of ice

TIP

DRILL AIR HOLES LATER
It's often easiest to drill the air holes and mouseholes while assembling the ice bar — when you know exactly where the holes should be.

Ready to Assemble . . .

Choose your ice bar's location. Assembling the bar on snow will make it easier to ensure that the bottom layer of lanterns is level and can be frozen to the ground. Create a good foundation by adding 2-3 shovelfuls of snow for each of the bar's supporting ice lantern towers. If you plan to add pieces of ice glass around the bar, you'll need extra snow to hold them in place, too.

Here is the ice bar layout (bird's-eye view):

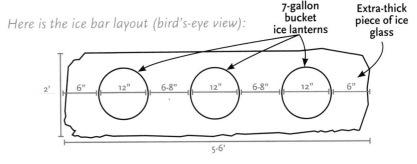

7-gallon bucket ice lanterns

Extra-thick piece of ice glass

2'   6"   12"   6-8"   12"   6-8"   12"   6"

5-6'

Here's the ice bar layout (side view):

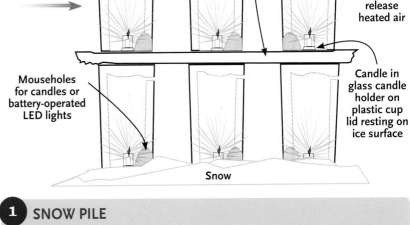

Thick ice glass

Bucket ice lantern

Wind direction

Drilled air holes to release heated air

Mouseholes for candles or battery-operated LED lights

Candle in glass candle holder on plastic cup lid resting on ice surface

Snow

1 SNOW PILE

Snow

STEP 1: Create a large pile of snow — about two heaping snow shovelfuls per bucket ice lantern tower.

② CREATE BASE LAYER

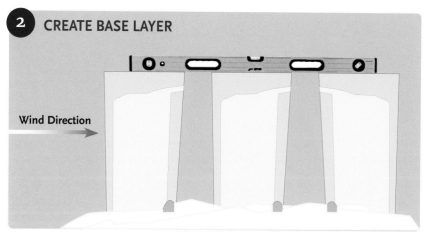

Wind Direction →

STEP 2: Position 3 of the bucket ice lanterns about 6"-8" apart in the snow pile. Place 2 lanterns so their mouseholes face away from the wind. Position the lantern farthest from the wind so its mousehole faces the other lanterns, effectively shielding all 3 from potential wind shifts.

Use snow to adjust lantern height. When a long level is placed across them, all lanterns should be the same height.

③ MOUSEHOLES

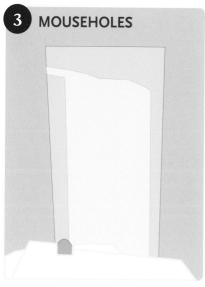

STEP 3: When the bucket ice lanterns are positioned securely, reach into each mousehole to clear away excess snow and create a level snow platform for each candle.

④ ADD FIRST ICE GLASS LAYER

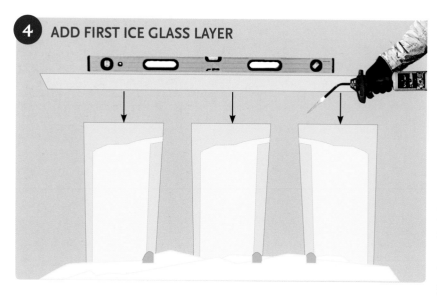

STEP 4: Position the smaller of the two sheets of thick ice glass over the three bucket lanterns. Use a long level to see if the top of the ice glass is level. If yes, remove the ice glass, torch the lantern tops to make them wet, and replace the ice glass. Let the ice pieces freeze together.

If the ice glass is not level, remove it and add ice chips or snow where needed. Then replace the ice glass and let the surfaces fuse together. If temps are colder than 8°F, freezing will be instantaneous. If temps are warmer, freezing will take an hour or so.

5 ADD NEXT LAYER OF LANTERNS AND ICE GLASS

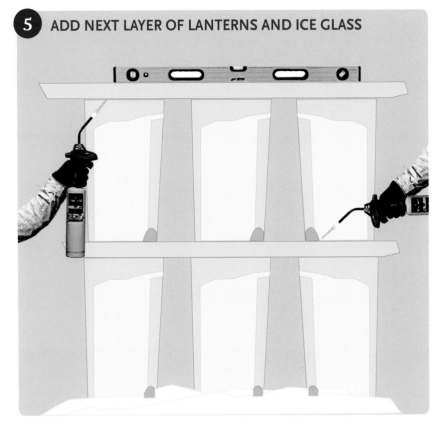

STEP 5: Add the next 3 bucket ice lanterns (all the same height) on top of the first ice glass sheet, placing them directly on top of the first three lanterns. Rotate 2 lanterns so their mouseholes face away from the wind. Rotate the lantern farthest from the wind so its mousehole faces the other lanterns, effectively shielding all 3 from potential wind shifts.

Make sure the bucket lanterns are even and level. Once they are, place the larger ice glass sheet on top of the lanterns. Check that the ice glass rests flat on all 3 lantern tops, adding snow/ice chips into any gaps. After leveling the ice glass, torch the underside so that lantern and ice glass surfaces become wet. Allow the ice components to freeze together.

6 PLACE AND LIGHT CANDLES

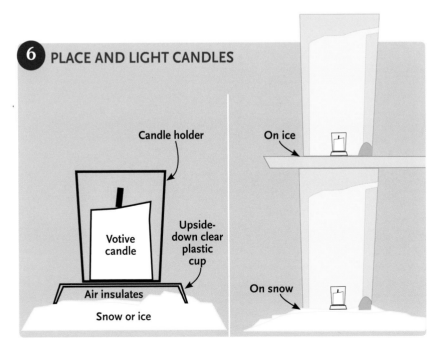

Candle holder

Votive candle

Upside-down clear plastic cup

Air insulates

Snow or ice

On ice

On snow

STEP 6: Through the mousehole of each lower bucket lantern, push an upside-down plastic cup into the snow. Place a votive candle in a candle holder on top of each cup. Light the candles.

Through the mousehole of each upper bucket lantern, place a short upside-down plastic cup onto the ice tabletop. Place a votive candle in a candle holder on top of each cup. Light the candles.

Light any other ice lanterns used as decorations.

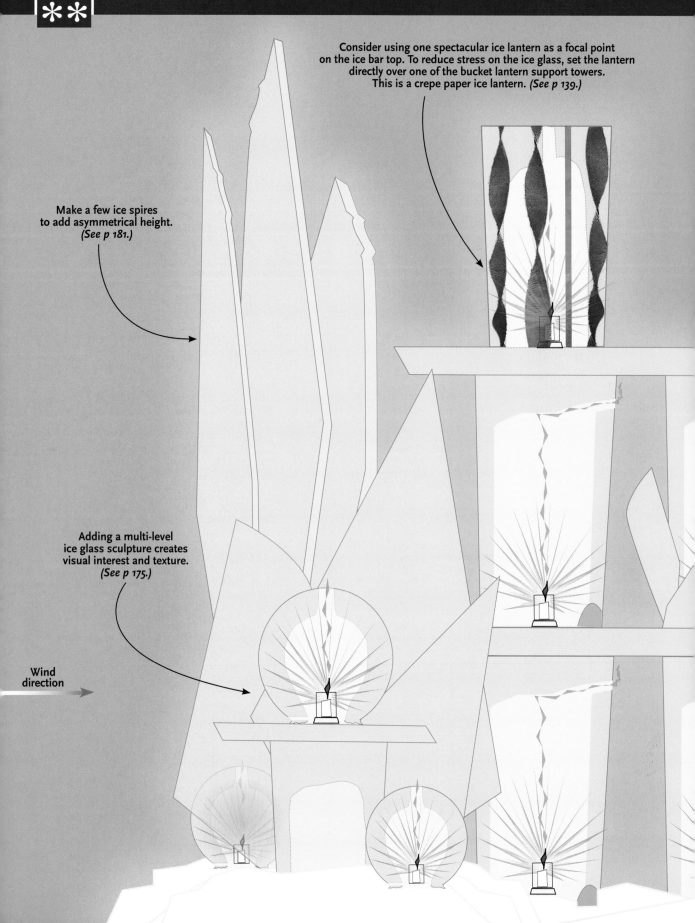

Consider using one spectacular ice lantern as a focal point on the ice bar top. To reduce stress on the ice glass, set the lantern directly over one of the bucket lantern support towers. This is a crepe paper ice lantern. *(See p 139.)*

Make a few ice spires to add asymmetrical height. *(See p 181.)*

Adding a multi-level ice glass sculpture creates visual interest and texture. *(See p 175.)*

Wind direction

Time to Decorate . . .

You can use the basic ice bar layout on page 193 just as it is — or jazz it up with ice flowers, ice spires and other ice pieces of any style, shape or size. When adding more ice as decoration, keep in mind that mouseholes must be shielded from wind and remain accessible for lighting and changing candles.

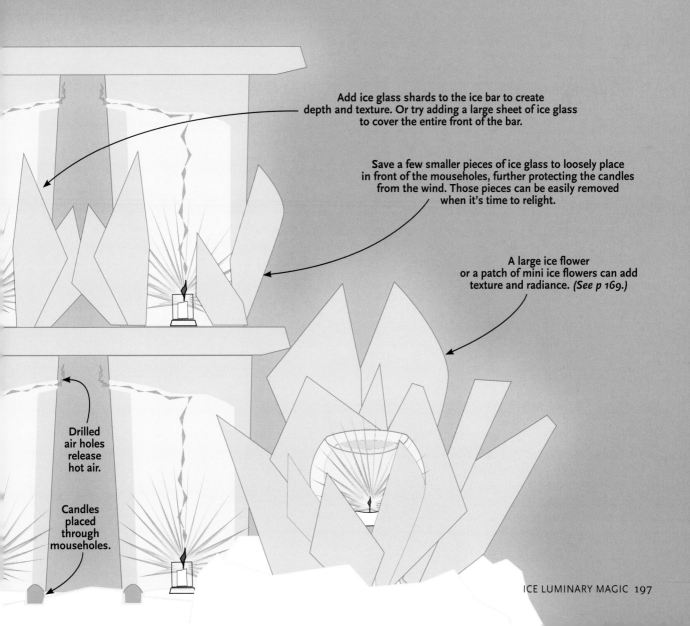

Add ice glass shards to the ice bar to create depth and texture. Or try adding a large sheet of ice glass to cover the entire front of the bar.

Save a few smaller pieces of ice glass to loosely place in front of the mouseholes, further protecting the candles from the wind. Those pieces can be easily removed when it's time to relight.

A large ice flower or a patch of mini ice flowers can add texture and radiance. *(See p 169.)*

Drilled air holes release hot air.

Candles placed through mouseholes.

With the camera held low to the snow,
this miniature ice castle looks gigantic.
Thank you to photographer and illustrator
Per Breiehagen for that helpful tip.
— Photo by Jennifer Shea Hedberg

✳✳ Miniature
✳✳ Ice Castle Lantern

The ice castle lantern is our final adventure because it incorporates so many of the techniques used in previous projects. It's essential to plan the layout before you begin — the scale and floor plan will be determined by the hard-to-find shapes and details. For example, it's tricky to find molds to make castle turrets. For this ice castle, I decided to use plastic champagne flutes as turret molds and designed everything else around that choice. For a larger castle, I make turrets using teardrop ice lanterns (see p 83) or large road-safety cones as molds.

Ice castle layout (bird's-eye view):

4" x 24" PVC pipe as the left castle bastion

2" x 24" PVC pipe as turret-topped towers

7" x 7" x 8" square-shaped container as the main castle chamber (Nonni's Biscotti or Twizzlers tubs)

4" x 24" PVC pipe as the right castle bastion

32 oz yogurt container as the second tier of the main castle chamber

1 MAKE ICE LANTERNS

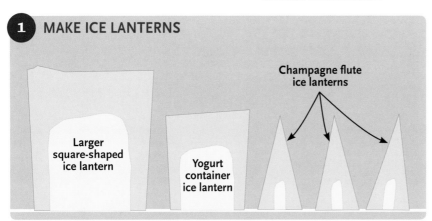

Larger square-shaped ice lantern

Yogurt container ice lantern

Champagne flute ice lanterns

STEP 1: Using the partial-freeze method found on page 19, create ice lanterns in the following molds:
- Nonni's Biscotti or Twizzlers square plastic container
- Yogurt container
- Plastic champagne flutes
  (Don't use glass flutes. They can break if the water freezes solid.)

WHAT YOU NEED

3 plastic champagne flutes

3 • 2" x 24" PVC pipes

2 • 4" x 24" PVC pipes

7" x 7" x 8" square-shaped plastic container (Nonni's Biscotti or Twizzlers tubs)

Yogurt container (32 oz)

Oscillating saw with 1.25" plunge blade

24" of bubble wrap

Level

Power drill and drill bits

A few handfuls of square-shaped ice cubes

Hot-tipped electrical tool (hot glue gun, soldering iron, stencil cutting tool, or leather brander)

Cold tap water

Snice *(see p 43)*

Cold temps or deep freezer

LED light or floating candle

2 MORE ICE LANTERNS

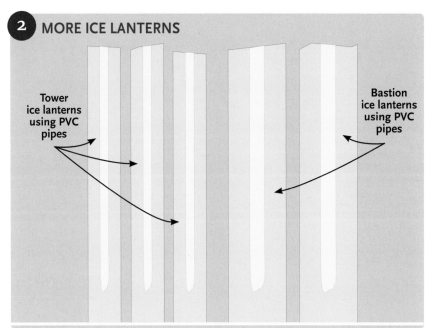

Tower ice lanterns using PVC pipes

Bastion ice lanterns using PVC pipes

TIP **MAKE EXTRAS**

Ice is a challenging medium. Mistakes happen. Just in case something goes wrong, it's wise to make extra ice castle pieces.

STEP 2: Using the *Open-Bottom Ice Lantern* (see p 35) technique, make lanterns for the ice castle towers.
- At least three 2" x 24" PVC pipes (These can freeze solid.)
- At least two 4" x 24" PVC pipes (Try not to freeze these solid.)

3 ANALYZE

STEP 3: Tops of ice lanterns are rarely completely flat. If you imagine assembling your unfinished building pieces into a castle, you'll be able to determine:
- which surfaces must be flattened.
- which pieces must be shortened.
- which pieces, if any, must be reshaped.

From this illustration, we can see that:
- the bastion ice lanterns, along with one tower ice lantern, must be shortened. *(See Step 4.)*
- all ice lantern tops and ice turret bottoms must be flattened.

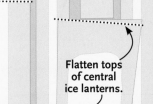

Flatten all turret tops

Shorten and flatten bottom section.

Shorten and flatten bastions.

Flatten tops of central ice lanterns.

4 SHORTEN ICE

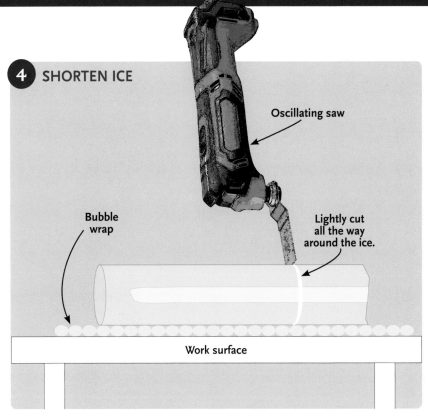

Oscillating saw

Bubble wrap

Lightly cut all the way around the ice.

Work surface

5 FLATTEN ENDS

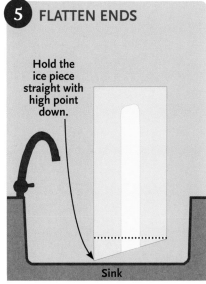

Hold the ice piece straight with high point down.

Sink

STEP 5: Fill a sink with hot water to warm the sink bottom, then drain. Angle the uneven end of the ice piece into the sink.

Hold it straight so the highest point hits first and starts to melt. Eventually, the uneven end will become flat.

Transfer the newly flattened ice piece to your work surface and double check it with a level.

STEP 4: Cut each ice piece that must be shortened. I use an oscillating saw to make such cuts, but it's also ok to use a Sawzall or a fine-tooth hand saw.

First, place the ice lantern on a piece of bubble wrap — a waterproof cushion on which to work.

To cut ice with the oscillating saw, start by lightly scoring exactly where you want to cut — just barely scratching the surface with the saw. Rotate the ice as you work. Deepen the scratch, then deepen it some more. Always go all the way around the ice piece.

Eventually the ice will break along the line you've created. When it does, you may need to flatten the cut end.

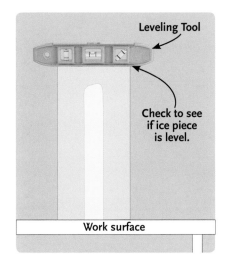

Leveling Tool

Check to see if ice piece is level.

Work surface

6 FLATTEN ALL

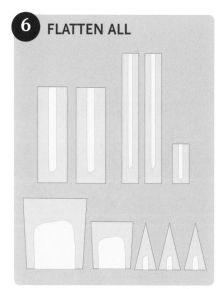

STEP 6: Continue shortening and flattening all the ice castle pieces, then wrap them in plastic and store them in below-freezing temps until ready for use.

7 STACK AND ASSESS

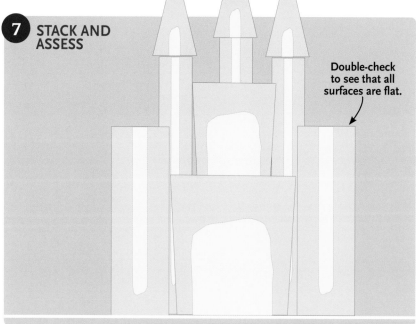

Double-check to see that all surfaces are flat.

STEP 7: When the ice pieces are cold and dry (so they don't stick together), assemble them to verify that they're straight and the correct height. *Hold on to the ice! Before the ice pieces are secured, they can fall and break.*

TIP

MAKE A MOUSEHOLE
Create a mousehole in the back of the main chamber so you can change the batteries of the LED lights. *(See p 184, Step 4.)*

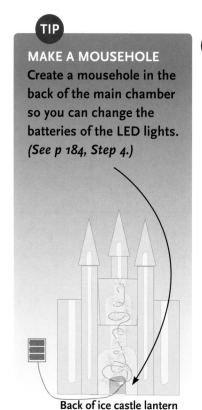

Back of ice castle lantern

8 LIGHTING STRATEGY

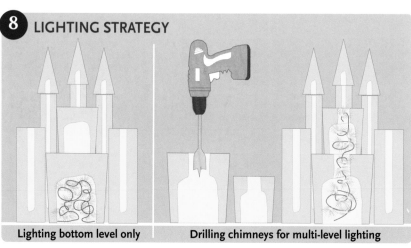

Lighting bottom level only | Drilling chimneys for multi-level lighting

STEP 8: With the ice pieces still assembled, work out your lighting strategy. A string of battery-operated, metal-wire LED lights in the main chamber of the ice castle will light it up brilliantly.

For more light, make a very large chimney in the top of the main chamber and a smaller chimney in the second tier so the light string can reach high into the castle. (For drilling info, *see p 166.*)

9 ADD EMBELLISHMENTS

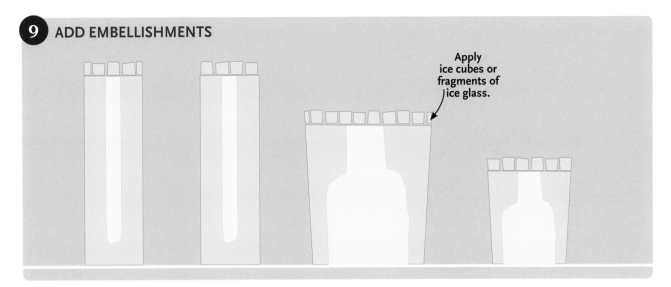

Apply ice cubes or fragments of ice glass.

STEP 9: Use the gluing technique from the *Ice Snowball Lantern* (*see p 110, Steps 3-4*) to add the square-shaped ice cubes to the tops of the bastions, second tier and main chamber. Let ice cubes freeze to ice castle pieces while vertical before wrapping the pieces in plastic and storing them in below-freezing temps.

10 JOIN SEGMENTS

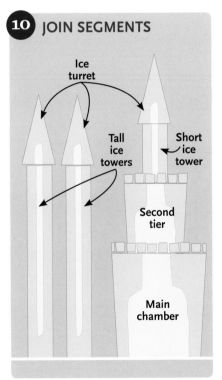

Ice turret

Tall ice towers

Short ice tower

Second tier

Main chamber

STEP 10:

Use the same technique to glue:
- the second tier to the top of the main chamber.
- the shortest ice tower to the top of the second tier.
- an ice turret to the short ice tower.
- the last 2 ice turrets to the ice towers.

Let all the pieces freeze together while vertical before wrapping them in plastic and storing them in below-freezing temps.

Ready to Display ...

With all the ice pieces finished, it's time to assemble them into an ice castle lantern for your own winter wonderland.

11 **FLAT WORK SURFACE**

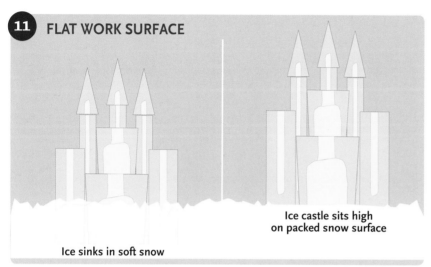

Ice castle sits high
on packed snow surface

Ice sinks in soft snow

12 **MAIN CHAMBER**

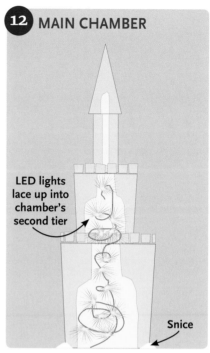

LED lights
lace up into
chamber's
second tier

Snice

STEP 11: Firmly pat down the snow where you plan to construct your ice castle. Add extra snow if necessary and pat down the area again so the snow surface is at the same level as the surrounding snow. After your castle is set up, you can landscape it with snow, bits of ice and small pine branches.

STEP 12: Stuff the end of a string of LED lights into the main chamber and push it into the second tier.

Position the lit main chamber in the center of your building area. Add a small amount of snice (*see p 43*) around the bottom where the ice chamber touches the snow.

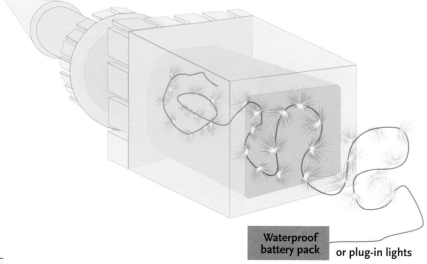

Waterproof
battery pack   or plug-in lights

13 ADD BASTIONS

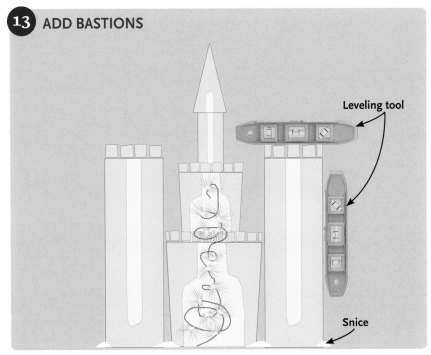

Leveling tool

Snice

STEP 13: Place the two bastions on the right and left sides of the main chamber. Use a leveling tool to make sure the ice is straight. Add snice around the bottoms where the bastions touch the snow.

14 ADD TURRETED TOWERS

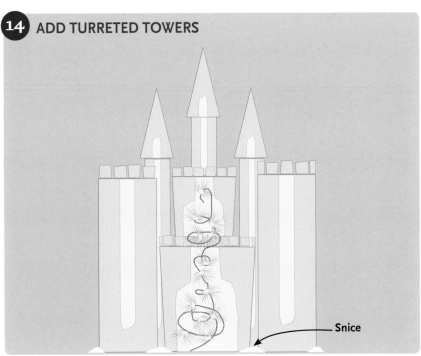

Snice

STEP 14: Place the two turreted towers behind the main chamber. Use the leveling tool. Add snice around the bottoms where the towers touch the snow.

15 GO CRAZY!

STEP 15: Of course, this floor plan is just the beginning. Think of all the plastic containers we use every day that could be re-purposed to make all sorts of ice shapes. Add rooms, fancy turrets, fences, walls — anything your heart desires.

If most of the ice is hollow or could surround a light source, every section can glow!

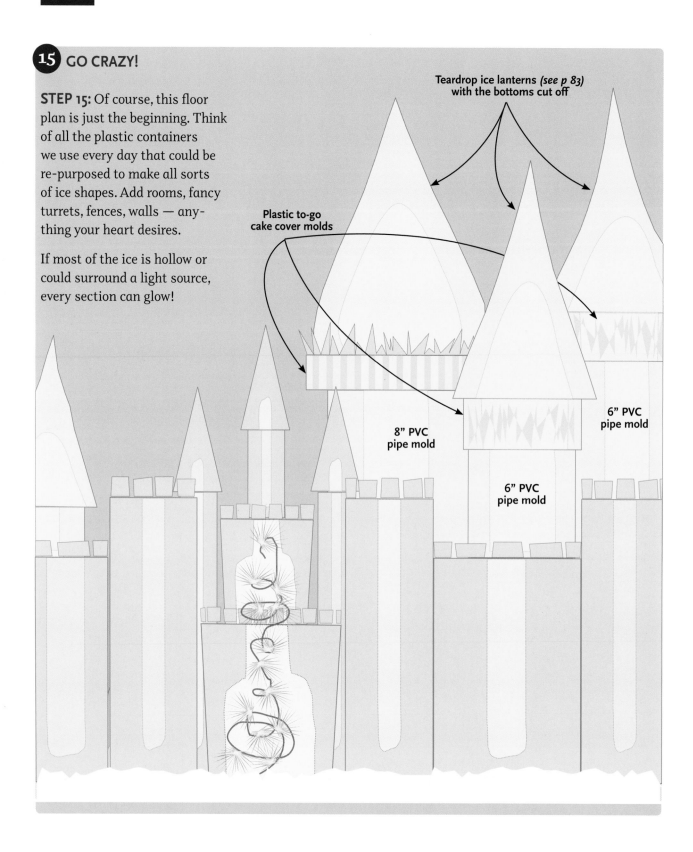

Teardrop ice lanterns *(see p 83)* with the bottoms cut off

Plastic to-go cake cover molds

8" PVC pipe mold

6" PVC pipe mold

6" PVC pipe mold

This larger ice castle — twice the size of the miniature version — was created to help illustrate The Polar Bear Wish, part of the Wish Book series by Lori Evert and Per Breiehagen.

— Photo by Jennifer Shea Hedberg

PART 5: Reflections

After years of experimenting with this mysterious substance we call ice,
I see more clearly than ever how its astonishing beauty connects us all.
I am grateful for the ingenuity of ice artists around the world,
for the generosity of photographers who have captured my work
— and for the realization that, in the stillness of a winter night,
all strangers are friends.

This magical piece of ice was created by spraying a fine mist of water
over a balloon in below-freezing temps so that long tendrils of ice formed
in stalagmite fashion. The balloon was removed to reveal a prehistoric-looking shell.
— Photo by Jennifer Shea Hedberg

Playing with Blue Light

When I first started building with ice, I rarely thought about how to capture my creations with a camera. But over the years, I've learned a lot about night photography from the experts who've stopped by to snap photos of my work. Now I always shoot with a tripod, a technique that reduces blur during long exposures. The most valuable tip I've ever received is to set up a camera before morning and evening twilight to take advantage of the special quality of light during the "blue hour." Sunlight through ice is stunning, but during the day's magical transition times the light of a candle and the architecture of ice are uniquely beautiful.

All photos on these page were taken during the blue hour. Clockwise from left: Faux butterflies and flowers captured in a bucket ice lantern. Close-up of an exquisitely textured bucket ice lantern. A thin, clear globe ice lantern holds evergreen twigs and a tiny snowman. Bucket ice lantern with multiple layers of star appliqués. Finnish glass bucket lanterns at the City of Lakes Luminary Loppet. Large ice castle lit with white LED lights in a client's front yard. Extra-large globe ice lantern near a festive winter firepit. — Photos by Jennifer Shea Hedberg

Ice, Fire and Community

Ice luminaries have a way of bringing people together. They speak of everything winter can be: a season for reflection and renewal, for adventure and discovery, for cultivating the close bonds of community. A mainstay of winter festivals around the world, ice lanterns also inspire people to create their own winter gatherings. A few years back my husband Tom and I started a pop-up ice luminary event almost by accident: We set up left-over ice projects at the creek near our home, lit them up and watched as passers-by exclaimed. With the help of many neighbors, the lark we soon named Middlemoon Creekwalk has become an annual tradition.

Clockwise from right: Kathy Loeffler builds an intricate ice castle in the Enchanted Forest of the City of Lakes Luminary Loppet in Minneapolis (photo by Jim Young). A gleaming ice castle at the Middlemoon Creekwalk on a snowy February evening (photo by Bob Hays). Children delight in ice princess toys frozen into globe ice lanterns (photo by Shane Foss). Youngsters explore an ice bar at the Middlemoon Creekwalk (photo by Martha Shull Archer). A family checks out a tall Finnish glass ice tower (photo by Larry Risser). A Nordic skier glides by a multi-leveled candlelit ice tower (photo by Bruce Challgren).

Ice Artists Everywhere

What I love most about sharing my ice artistry with the world is that people reciprocate. I've received notes and photos from people all around the globe who've been playing with ice for years or who've just caught the bug. By nature, ice artists are inventors and experimenters — we discover what ice can do and then challenge ourselves to shape it into new kinds of loveliness. It's an enterprise that keeps us always and forever connected. I hope we will continue to share.

Clockwise from left: David Falk creates towering ice triangles in his Winnipeg front yard (photo by Kalyn Falk). Lauri Hohman of Silver Bay, Minnesota, captured this playful image of stacked ice lanterns lit by the sun. Mary Arneson of Minneapolis, a longtime contributor to the Middlemoon Creekwalk, created an ingenious bucket ice lantern with ice people fishing through the chimney hole (photo by Bob Hays). Becky Stolinas of Rio, Wisconsin, makes brilliant ice constructions — including this gift-wrapped cube of ice. Mark Clingan of Minneapolis turned a globe ice lantern into a shrimp bowl lit with LED lights. Gail Murton of Finland, Minnesota, gets rave reviews for her globe ice lantern re-purposed into a bird feeder. And don't forget to check out Pat Palanuk, also of Winnipeg, whose photos of ice forms lit by the sun can be found on page 60. Thanks to all for sharing your art!

Dream, play, experiment . . .

Use this space to keep notes as you explore the ice universe.
Please share your discoveries! Email me at jennifer@icewrangler.com.
Check out my blog and social media links at icewrangler.com.
#icewrangler #iceluminarymagic

METRIC CONVERSIONS

TEMPERATURE

Fahrenheit	Celsius
32	0
25	-3.9
20	-6.7
15	-9.4
10	-12.2
5	-15.0
0	-17.8
-5	-20.6
-10	-23.3
-15	-26.1
-20	-28.0
-25	-31.7
-30	-34.4

LENGTH

Inches	Centimeters
1/4	0.6
3/8	1.0
1/2	1.3
1	2.5
2	5.1
3	7.6
4	10.2
5	12.7
6	15.2
7	17.8
8	20.3
9	22.9
10	25.4
11	28.0
12 (1 ft)	30.5

Feet	Meters
1 (12 in)	0.3
2	0.6
3	0.9
4	1.2
5	1.5
6	1.8
7	2.1
8	2.4
9	2.7
10	3.0
11	3.4
12	3.7

VOLUME

1 ounce	30 ml
15 ounces	443 ml
32 ounces	946 ml
2.5 pints	1.2 L
1 gallon	3.8 L
2 gallons	7.6 L
2.5 gallons	9.5 L
5 gallons	18.9 L
6 gallons	22.7 L
7 gallons	26.5 L

PROJECT	DATE	TIME	SIZE (WEIGHT)	OUTCOME

DISCLAIMER: Ice is slippery, cold and heavy. Working with it can dangerous.
Use caution, care and good judgment when following the procedures in this book.
Follow the instructions and safety precautions associated with the book's projects and with the various tools
and materials described. While every effort has been made to ensure the accuracy of the information within,
the author and publisher disclaim any liability to any party for any loss, injury, damage,
or disruption caused as a result of the contents of this book.

Ice Luminary Magic: The Ice Wrangler's Guide to Making Illuminated Ice Creations
© 2018 Jennifer Shea Hedberg • Text & Illustrations © Jennifer Shea Hedberg
Photographs copyright individual photographers as noted. All others © Jennifer Shea Hedberg
Front cover photo © Martha Shull Archer. Back cover photo bottom right ©Bob Hays.
Book design by Jennifer Shea Hedberg

Chief Editors: Kate Stanley & Tom Hedberg with additional editing assistance by Kat Shea, Ellen Van Iwaarden,
Dave Schaenzer, Susan Lenfestey, Mary Arneson, Dale Hammerschmidt, and Peter Hedberg.

Thank you to Per Breiehagen and Nat Case for photo editing assistance.

Published in 2018 by Wintercraft®.
Wintercraft.com

For information about wholesale discounts, premiums, and bulk purchases,
please visit Wintercraft.com.

The author and publisher do not market, endorse, or are affiliated in any way
with other products and brands listed herein.

Library of Congress Cataloging-in-Publication Data available upon request.

ISBN 978-1-59353-068-6

First Edition

Printed in Canada